CONCENTRATION AND PRICE-COST MARGINS IN MANUFACTURING INDUSTRIES

CONCENTRATION AND PRICE-COST MARGINS IN MANUFACTURING INDUSTRIES

Norman R. Collins and
Lee E. Preston

PUBLICATIONS OF
THE INSTITUTE OF BUSINESS AND ECONOMIC RESEARCH
UNIVERSITY OF CALIFORNIA

UNIVERSITY OF CALIFORNIA PRESS
Berkeley and Los Angeles: 1968

University of California Press
 Berkeley and Los Angeles, California
Cambridge University Press
 London, England

Copyright © 1968, by The Regents of the University of California
Library of Congress Catalog Card Number: 68–63025
Printed in the United States of America

For Dolores and Patricia

Preface

This study examines the relationship between conventional measures of industrial concentration and the percentage margin between prices and costs. Much has been written about the relationships that may be expected between industry structure and economic performance, and a great variety of indicators and measures may be used to examine these relationships empirically. Concentration data, which report the share of a specified small number of firms in the total activity of an industry, have become the most widely available structural indicators, but controversy has continued as to their interpretive or predictive significance. Therefore, our intention here is to examine the usefulness of concentration indexes as predictors of interindustry differences in price-cost margins.

Simply stated, the proposition under analysis here is that the level of concentration affects the interdependence of action among firms and, therefore, the closeness of their market performance to the theoretical monopoly solution. The hypothesis for statistical investigation is that the relative excess of prices over costs is higher in more highly concentrated industries than in less concentrated ones. In testing this hypothesis, it is necessary, of course, to consider some of the other variables that might be associated with interindustry differences in price-cost margins. However, we have attempted to keep the hypothesis simple and the number of explanatory variables few in order to utilize the largest possible collection of data and to obtain results that are easily interpreted. In general, our results, taken in conjunction with those of previous studies based on more limited collections of data, support the conclusion that the level of measured concentration is associated with interindustry differences in profitability, although an important portion of these differences remains to be explained by other factors.

We are indebted to a large number of our colleagues for advice and criticism during the period we have been working on this study. Professor Leonard W. Weiss provided us with many helpful suggestions in his careful review of the manuscript. Professor James N. Boles gave us frequent counsel on the statistical and computer operations involved in the empirical work. We are indebted to the authors whose works are reported in Chapter II for their review of our presentation of their findings. Our thanks are also due to Mrs. Judith Drake for her diligent work in the assembly and processing of the industry data and to Mrs. Ellen McGibbon for her assistance in the typing of the various drafts of the manuscript. Financial support for this project was received from the Research Program in Marketing of the Graduate School of Business Administration and the Department of Agricultural Economics, University of California, Berkeley.

Contents

LIST OF TABLES

LIST OF FIGURES

I

Industry Structure and Performance Results

Both economic theory and industrial experience suggest that the structural features of an industry strongly influence the competitive interaction among its constituent firms and the prices, profits, and output levels resulting in its markets. Only under rather narrowly specified theoretical conditions, however, has it been possible to deduce market performance entirely from structural factors. Indeed, beyond the limiting cases of complete monopoly and perfect competition, theory appears to serve best as a guide to the identification of potentially significant variables and to the development of hypotheses. These hypotheses have been investigated primarily on a case-by-case basis in industry studies and occasionally in collections of cross-sectional data developed for special analytical purposes.[1]

The accumulation of cross-sectional data in the form of concentration statistics—shares of the *n* largest firms in some aggregate of economic activity—has not, however, generally reflected an attempt to examine functional hypotheses. Such data have been computed for manufacturing industries in the United States periodically since 1935. Tabulations of data for 1954 and 1958 show the shares of the largest firms in the total value of shipments and total employment in their

---

[1] Important examples of the latter are: Joe S. Bain, *Barriers to New Competition* (Cambridge, Massachusetts: Harvard University Press, 1956). Edwin Mansfield, "Entry, Innovation, and the Growth of Firms," *American Economic Review*, Vol. LII, No. 5 (December, 1962), pp. 1023–1051.

industries and in the total value of shipments of individual classes of products.[2]

A great part of the discussion of these data has been directed toward the descriptive content of the numbers themselves and the interindustry and time trends revealed in them. Such discussion tends to treat the numerical results as of intrinsic interest, or at least of known significance. Valuable as much of this work has been in developing and improving available economic information, much uncertainty remains as to the meaning to be attached to the facts discovered. This uncertainty is reflected in the quotations from authorities assembled by the U.S. Chamber of Commerce,[3] and is well summarized by the remark of Professor Kaysen that simple concentration measures "can point to the existence of markets in which the presence and effects of oligopoly deserve detailed study; no more sophisticated measure calculable *without* such detailed study of the particular market can do any more."[4]

The investigation reported in this monograph was undertaken in an attempt to clarify the significance of concentration data as a guide to price and price-cost behavior in industrial markets. Much of the manufacturing output in the United States originates in industries in which a few large firms account for a high percentage of total assets, employment, and sales. However, the relative importance of any small number of large firms varies from industry to industry, and in most industries has changed substantially over time. Within this context we raise the following question: Can

---

[2] U.S. Congress, Senate, Subcommittee on Antitrust and Monopoly, Committee on the Judiciary, *Concentration in American Industry*, 85th Cong., 1st Sess., 1957. *Idem, Concentration Ratios in Manufacturing Industry, 1958*, Parts I and II, 87th Cong., 2d Sess., 1962.

[3] U.S. Chamber of Commerce, *The Significance of Concentration Ratios*, No. 1, Reports on Measurement of Economic Concentration (Washington, 1957).

[4] Carl Kaysen, Comment on "Economic Theory and the Measurement of Concentration," by Tibor Scitovsky, *Business Concentration and Price Policy* (Princeton: Princeton University Press, 1955), p. 117.

differences in the relative importance of large firms among industries, as measured by concentration data, contribute substantially to the explanation of interindustry differences in price-cost margins and profits?

Many of the discussions of concentration data appear to presume that the answer to this question is affirmative. Statements are made to the effect that highly concentrated industries lack the structural conditions which make competitive behavior possible; therefore they cannot fail to approximate the textbook monopoly result. In contrast, it is frequently argued that patterns of market conduct in concentrated industries yield market performance results not substantially different from those that would arise under large-numbers competitive conditions. With a few notable exceptions, systematic examination of the concentration data has not been directed toward the resolution of these issues.

STRUCTURE-PERFORMANCE RELATIONSHIPS

Market structure occupies a strategic role in conventional price theory. The behavior of hypothetical firms with respect to prices, costs, levels of output, and profits is explained or predicted on the basis of deductions from certain given or assumed conditions, including those describing the structure of the markets within which the firms are operating. The entire theoretical apparatus is built on certain basic assumptions about the behavior of buyers, the motivations of sellers, the internal organization of firms, and the technology of production. Additional factors are required, however, to explain differential experience among firms and industries. As Bain points out:

> . . . Market structure may logically be expected (and is observed) to influence the conduct of firms in maximizing profits, the interaction of the conduct of competing firms in the same market, and the end performance emerging from the industry. In brief, market structure affects the character

and intensity of competition among firms in the same industry, and thus the conduct and performance of these firms.[5]

Both structure and performance are multidimensional concepts. Thus it may be true that some structural attributes may be shown to be directly associated with some performance outcomes, and simultaneously true that other structure and performance variables are unrelated or associated in the opposite way. The principal market structure features include number and relative size distribution of buyers and sellers, condition of entry, extent of product differentiation, geographical market structure, and long- and short-run cost conditions. Performance dimensions include production efficiency, output levels and rates of growth, price-cost relationships and profit rates, speed and character of technological change, and resource conservation. Both theoretical argument and empirical evidence can be adduced to explain a variety of possible relationships among this complex of variables.

A number of recent contributions have increased our ability to analyze some of these relationships at the purely theoretical level.[6] However, it is generally agreed that new and more precise generalizations as to expected patterns of structure-performance relationships require continued empirical research. Empirical studies would hopefully produce results not only of academic interest but also of importance for the development of public policies and the conduct of business management. Bain has pointed out that, in "an economy

---

[5] Bain, *Industrial Organization* (New York: John Wiley & Sons, Inc., 1959), pp. 27–28.
[6] G. J. Stigler, "A Theory of Oligopoly," *Journal of Political Economy,* Vol. LXXII, No. 1 (February, 1964), pp. 44–61. Martin Shubik, *Strategy and Market Structure: Competition, Oligopoly and the Theory of Games* (New York: John Wiley & Sons, Inc., 1959), esp. Chaps. 10 and 11. R. L. Bishop, "Duopoly: Collusion or Warfare?" *American Economic Review,* Vol. L, No. 5 (December, 1960), pp. 933–961. W. J. Baumol, *Business Behavior, Value and Growth* (New York: Macmillan Co., 1959), Part I, Chaps. 2–8.

where technological and other factors make any close approximation to pure and perfect competition substantially unattainable, it is important for purposes of policy to know in what kinds of imperfect markets competitive behavior will be reasonably compatible with a viable capitalism and will reasonably enhance general economic welfare." [7] The literature of workable competition [8] suggests certain, often subjective, standards that might be used in appraising industry performance. Relevant as these standards may be, greater objectivity in method and firmer grounding in empirical evidence are to be desired.

CONCENTRATION AS A PREDICTIVE VARIABLE

Concentration—the percentage share of the n largest firms in the total activity (sales, employment, capacity, etc.)—on the selling side of a market is but one of several potentially significant structural variables. However, examination of the predictive significance of this variable is well justified at the present state of our knowledge of market relationships, for a number of reasons. First, the assumption that the concentration data are of predictive or interpretive significance, an assumption necessary to justify the substantial cost and effort required simply to obtain them, calls for empirical examination. Second, concentration data are probably the most widely available indexes of industry structure; if they are of strong predictive significance, the need for additional and less easily obtained information is reduced, and vice versa. Third, in much theoretical discussion, con-

---

[7] Bain, "Workable Competition in Oligopoly: Theoretical Considerations and Some Empirical Evidence," *American Economic Review*, Vol. XL, No. 2 (May, 1950), p. 35.
[8] J. M. Clark, "Toward a Concept of Workable Competition," *American Economic Review*, Vol. XXX, No. 2 (June, 1940), pp. 241–256. J. W. Markham, "An Alternative Approach to the Concept of Workable Competition," *American Economic Review*, Vol. XL, No. 3 (June, 1950), pp. 349–362.

centration has come to serve as a proxy term for the degree of oligopoly, with the argument, expressed or implied, that the greater the degree of oligopoly, the greater the ease of oligopolistic coördination, and thus the closer market performance results will be to the monopoly solution.

This chain of thought is reflected in Scitovsky's well-known paper.[9] Referring specifically to the interpretation of concentration data, he states:

> Measures of concentration try to express the number and size distribution of competitors in terms of a one-parameter index, which could then be regarded as a direct measure of the degree of oligopoly.[10]
>
> When oligopolists sell at prices above marginal cost and oligopsonists buy at prices below marginal value, relative prices become unreliable as indexes of relative scarcities and relative demands; and the producers, whose policies are guided by market prices, may make socially undesirable decisions. In particular, too little will be produced and too few resources utilized in industries with high margins; and too much will be produced and too many resources utilized in industries with low margins.[11]

The same point has been made by Bain in terms of profit rates:

> . . . There will be larger profit rates with higher seller concentration than with moderate or low seller concentration if we posit a systematic association between the probability of effective collusion and the degree of seller concentration within an industry.[12]

---

[9] Tibor Scitovsky, "Economic Theory and the Measurement of Concentration," *Business Concentration and Price Policy* (Princeton: Princeton University Press, 1955), pp. 101–113.

[10] *Ibid.*, p. 109.

[11] *Ibid.*, p. 104.

[12] Bain, "Relation of Profit Rate to Industry Concentration: American Manufacturing, 1936–1940," *Quarterly Journal of Economics*, Vol. LXV, No. 3 (August, 1951), pp. 295–296.

Moderate concentration, it may be argued, should tend to give rise to quasi-competitive market behavior—imperfect collusion, kinked demand curve conformations, and the sporadic appearance of chaotic competition—whereas high concentration should provide an environment conducive to effective collusion or its equivalent. This hypothesis essentially rests on the premise and argument that, given the incentive to joint profit maximization, the impediments to express or tacit agreement increase, while the restraint of recognized interdependence on independent price cutting should decrease (with ordinary frictions and imperfections) as concentration decreases, and at such a rate that a shift in competitive pattern results over a certain concentration zone within oligopoly.[13]

Such a view of the concentration measure would lead us to expect that market performance is fairly closely related to the power relation among firms and hence to concentration if this power relation "depends largely" on the size distribution of firms. This view is not uniformly held, however. In commenting on Scitovsky's paper, Kaysen stated:

The premise of this argument—that the power relation depends chiefly on the number and size distribution of competing sellers—must be denied. Many other features of the market are relevant to this "power relation." At least the following are of equal importance with the number and size distribution of sellers in many market situations: the rate of growth of demand over time, the character and speed of technological change, the degree to which sellers operate in other markets, the extent and nature of product differentiation, and the goals of individual firm policy—e.g., profit maximization vs. security.[14]

On the basis of this reasoning Kaysen concluded: "It seems vain to expect that numbers and size distribution alone will

---

[13] *Idem*, "Workable Competition in Oligopoly . . . ," p. 44.
[14] Kaysen, *op. cit.*, p. 118.

explain market behavior, and therefore equally vain to hope
for more from concentration measures than that they should
provide a preliminary basis on which resources for further
study should be allocated." [15] His suggestion was to proceed
with more studies of particular markets and further elabora-
tion of oligopoly theory.

THE PRESENT STUDY: MODEL AND HYPOTHESIS

The preceding comments indicate that there is far from
general agreement as to the expected association between
seller concentration and particular indicators of market performance. All parties appear to be agreed, however, that
both theoretical and empirical work will be required to clarify these relationships. We have chosen to examine in detail
the hypothesis that the index of seller concentration is directly associated with interindustry differences in the ratio
of prices to variable costs, as well as with more familiar
indicators of profitability.

The logic of our analysis may be set forth in the following
sequence:

1. In theory, given the cost structure of the firm and the
market demand, prices are higher and price-cost margins
wider under conditions of monopoly (single seller) than
under conditions of competition (many sellers, free entry).
If we define total costs to include normal profit, then we
would expect the revenue-cost ratio to have a minimum
value of unity for competitive firms, and to reach an upper
limit, determined by the cost and demand conditions, in a
single-firm monopoly. If only direct or current costs are
included, then the minimum ratio, greater than one, would
indicate the gross margin necessary to generate "normal"
profits on capital.

2. In order to use revenue-cost ratios computed from

---

[15] *Ibid.*

available data as indicators of the closeness of industry performance to the theoretical extremes of monopoly or competition, two important conditions must be met:

a) Capital costs must be considered as well as current costs, and average variable costs must be assumed constant and equal to marginal costs in each industry. Available large-scale cross-sectional data contain industry totals for current, but not capital, costs. Thus the revenue-cost ratio computed from these data approximates the ratio of price to average variable cost and reflects the gross, rather than the net, profit margin. The same gross margin might be associated with very different price-marginal cost and profit-capital relationships in industries with different cost structures. If rates of return on capital were equalized among industries, the ratio of profits to current costs would be higher in more capital-intensive industries.

It might be argued that differences in capital requirements are not relevant to the *identification* of an association between industry structure and price-cost margins in the short run. Such margins are wide because buyers are willing to pay particular prices rather than go without the product. High capital requirements do not, in the short run, *cause* high profit margins; costs will not be covered by revenues simply because they have been incurred. However, the theoretical proposition under examination here deals with equilibrium adjustments, not unstable short-run situations. Therefore, the possibility must be considered that differences in the current price-cost margins in various industries are requisite for the attainment of equal "normal" rates of profit on the capital employed over the long run. In this analysis, differences in capital requirements among industries are specifically taken into account.

b) The elasticity of final market demand must be the same in all cases or, as an alternative, the relationship between the elasticity of demand of the firm and the concentration index must be the same. Under conditions of monopoly, the ratio of marginal cost to price is a function of the elasticity of demand. This implies that, for horizontal average variable (= marginal) cost functions, the greater the elasticity of market demand, the less the percentage margin between price and average variable cost (and the less the ratio of total revenue to total variable cost). Thus, we might find two monopolized industries with different price-cost ratios owing to differences in the elasticity of final demand.

To avoid this complication we might assume that industry demand functions are equally elastic within the relevant range. If this were true, then, for a given cost structure, an industry with a higher revenue-cost ratio would more closely approach the monopoly performance result than would an industry with a lower ratio. Lerner used this conception to formulate his well-known index of the degree of monopoly:

$$\frac{\text{price} - \text{marginal cost}}{\text{price}}$$

He did not use this index to develop empirical tests of the association between observed market conditions and "monopoly" market performance; rather, he identified it as a summary indicator of the impact of monopoly on prices and therefore upon the allocation of resources.[16]

An alternative assumption justifying the same comparison is that the elasticity of demand relevant to individual firms in an industry is affected only by their own numbers and relative market shares, not (except in the limiting monopoly case) by the elasticity of total market demand. This alternative is tenable under any of a number of possible chains of reasoning, including that associated with the concept of the kinked demand curve. Scattered empirical results might be drawn upon to support such a hypothesis; however, we do not argue it here but simply cite it as a logical possibility.

---

[16] A. P. Lerner, "The Concept of Monopoly and the Measurement of Monopoly Power," *Review of Economic Studies*, Vol. 1, Nos. 1–3 (1933–34), pp. 157–175.

Major portions of our analysis are based upon a priori industry groupings intended to provide a foundation for the assumption that demand conditions are not substantially different among the industries in each grouping. In other parts of the analysis this issue may be relevant to the interpretation of results; that is, one may ask whether the interindustry differences observed are such as might be anticipated on the basis of differences in demand conditions alone.

3. Just as industry performance may, under certain assumptions, be ranked along a scale from monopoly profits at one extreme to competitive normal profits at the other, so industry structures may be ranked along a similar scale from single-firm monopoly to large-numbers competition. One basis for such an ordering is a concentration index, the share of the n largest units in the total industry activity. Any such one-parameter indicator is, of course, deficient in some respects. One serious deficiency in concentration data may be a failure to reflect the magnitude and strength of foreign competition.

4. The final element in our argument concerns the industry or market classifications within which concentration, cost, and revenue are measured. Categorization of economic phenomena is not a simple task, especially for data dealing with market competition, since markets overlap and interact in a variety of ways.[17] Statistical reporting demands a classification system composed of mutually exclusive categories that are, in total, exhaustive. Although ideally we might wish to construct theoretically significant industries and original tabulations of their characteristics from basic sources, as a practical matter we are mainly constrained to

---

[17] James W. McKie, "Industry Classification and Sector Measures of Industrial Production," U.S. Bureau of the Census Working Paper No. 20 (Washington, 1965). Maxwell R. Conklin and Harold T. Goldstein, "Census Principles of Industry and Product Classification, Manufacturing Industries," *Business Concentration and Price Policy* (Princeton: Princeton University Press, 1955), pp. 15–55.

use groupings based on the Standard Industrial Classification (SIC).

The differing geographical scope of markets in various industries poses a problem also. In many industries, the presence of multiplant firms and nationwide distribution practices makes the nationwide concentration index an appropriate measure of seller concentration in most markets. In other cases, however, the dominance of regional markets by regional firms may seriously alter the picture. Geographic concentration indexes are available for only a small number of industries.[18] Rather than rely on this limited collection of data, we have constructed a crude index of regionality to take account of this type of interindustry difference.

5. We are now able to summarize the hypothesis under examination in this study. Interindustry differences in the relationship between revenues and costs will be positively associated with the degree of oligopoly, as reflected in a concentration index, when differences in capital requirements and the relative importance of regional versus national markets are taken into account. Other things being equal, the share of a small number of large firms in the total activity of an industry is a predictor of the closeness of market revenue-cost results to those that would be associated with theoretical monopoly conditions.

Should such a predictor be expected to operate as a continuous function or only between discrete categories? The received body of theory is somewhat ambiguous on this point. If the major theoretical proposition is the distinction between price behavior under tight oligopoly and all other forms of market structure—as the preceding quotation from Bain seems to suggest—the relevant empirical question is the direction and significance of differences in revenue-cost relations between highly concentrated industries and all

---

[18] U.S. Congress, Senate, Subcommittee on Antitrust and Monopoly, Committee on the Judiciary, *Concentration Ratios* . . . , Part II.

other industries. If, on the contrary, a continuous structural spectrum ranging from large-group monopolistic competition to tight oligopoly is recognized, then the presence of a continuous function relating this structural spectrum to performance variables should be investigated. The latter possibility is suggested by Scitovsky's comment, previously quoted, on the "degree of oligopoly." The theory of oligopoly is not at present so complete, even at the purely formal level, that we may unequivocally describe either the discrete or the continuous hypothesis as *the* theoretical expectation. Both are worthy of analysis.

THE REVENUE-COST RELATION

The dependent variable selected for analysis in this study is the difference between revenues and current costs, expressed as a percentage of revenues. This statistic is closely related to Lerner's measure of the degree of monopoly. However, our statistic is computed from aggregate data and does not exclude capital costs; thus it does not bear any direct correspondence to the long-run marginal cost-price comparison suggested by Lerner. We describe our computed statistic as the percentage gross margin over costs, or simply the margin.[19]

The measure we have chosen is only one of many possible indicators of industry profitability. We have chosen it both because it is most closely related to the theoretical predictions under examination and because it can be computed for a large sample of industries. Profits in relation to capital or net worth (i.e., rates of return) are more frequently made the subjects of detailed investigation, and we compare our own measures with available rate-of-return data. However,

---

[19] Hultgren used this concept in his recent study of business profits; however, his margin figures were developed from FTC-SEC data. Thor Hultgren, *Cost, Prices, and Profits: Their Cyclical Relations* (New York: Columbia University Press, 1965), Chap. 1.

the computation of rate-of-return data for this purpose requires as many and as difficult arbitrary adjustments and assumptions as does the margin measure.[20] In addition, the available data do not permit accurate computation of rates of return for most of the industrial classifications for which accurate concentration data exist.

Some qualifications to the general usage of reported cost, revenue, and profit data as evidence of departures from competitive conditions should be noted. Besides the industry demand and cost structure differences mentioned above, there are four important factors that require brief comment: (1) the short-run nature of the observations; (2) the possible dangers involved in averaging; (3) the possible existence of monopoly costs or "expense preferences"; and (4) the goals of oligopolistic firms.

High profits, particularly if found in single short-run observations, may reflect the initial stages of competitive adjustment rather than relatively stable monopolistic conditions. Thus, analysis of profits as evidence of differences in competitive conditions among industries may be inappropriate if these industries differ widely in the rate and direction of demand changes, technological progress, or broad institutional setting. The likelihood of this error may be reduced through the analysis of industries grouped according to a priori similarities in these dimensions.

The hypothesized relationship between concentration and average industry price-cost margins might prove empirically to hold as a result of two different sets of conditions. Consider two industries, each composed of large and small firms but differing in the relative importance of each. Average industry margins might be higher in that industry in which the larger firms account for a greater share of sales, either (a) because the larger firms hold a price umbrella over the

[20] Bain, "The Profit Rate as a Measure of Monopoly Power," *Quarterly Journal of Economics*, Vol. LV, No. 2 (February, 1941), pp. 271–293.

market or (b) because the larger firms alone tend to have higher margins, yielding a positive relationship between concentration and price-cost margins as these firms are given heavier weight in the industry average.[21] Which, if either, of these conditions may prevail is an important and interesting question; however, we regard it as subsidiary to the primary question of whether industry structure and average levels of price-cost margins are related.

The widened range of managerial discretion associated with positions of market power may result in increases in certain types of expenses and emoluments within the firm rather than, or as well as, in reported profits. Stigler has argued the existence of monopoly gains in the payments to factors of production other than capital and has commented that "the magnitude of monopoly elements in wages, executive compensation, royalties, and rents is possibly quite large." [22] The possible association between concentration and labor earnings has been investigated by Weiss using data from a sample of the 1960 Census of Population.[23] He

---

[21] Bain's analysis of profit rates for his industry sample found "no statistically significant general relation of size [of firm] to profits." Bain, "Relation of Profit Rate . . . ," p. 306. See also: Stigler, *Capital and Rates of Return in Manufacturing Industries* (Princeton: Princeton University Press, 1963). H. O. Stekler, *Profitability and Size of Firm,* Institute of Business and Economics Research Special Publications (Berkeley: University of California Press, 1963). Howard J. Sherman, *Macrodynamic Economics* (New York: Appleton-Century-Crofts, 1964), Chap. 8.
  Results recently reported by Blair show that, for 290 large firms distributed among thirty different manufacturing industries, there was no tendency for the rate of return (1959–1963) to be associated with size rank within the relevant industry. He did, however, note that low or negative rates of return were extremely rare among these large firms. U.S. Congress, Senate, Subcommittee on Antitrust and Monopoly, Committee on the Judiciary, *Hearings, Pursuant to S. Res. 40, Economic Concentration,* 89th Cong., 1st Sess., 1965, "Part 4. Concentration and Efficiency," pp. 1551–1555. (Statement of John M. Blair, Chief Economist, Subcommittee on Antitrust and Monopoly.)
[22] Stigler, "The Statistics of Monopoly and Merger," *Journal of Political Economy,* Vol. LXIV, No. 1 (February, 1956), p. 35.
[23] L. W. Weiss, "Concentration and Labor Earnings," *American Economic Review,* Vol. LVI, No. 1 (March, 1966), pp. 96–117. Weiss' results are strongly affected by the extent of unionization. For his most general sub-

found that workers in given occupations do receive higher incomes in concentrated than in unconcentrated industries. However, these earnings differences could be accounted for entirely by differences in personal characteristics that affect the quality or suitability of labor. Thus, the observed tendency is for concentrated industries to use a portion of their potential profits to hire "superior" labor (or to be pressed by unionization to pay higher wages, which in turn attract "superior" labor). Other possible ways in which potential profits may be transformed into increased expenditures were suggested by Williamson in his analysis of managerial "expense preference." He emphasized that "managers do not have a neutral attitude toward all classes of expenses. Instead, some types of expenses have positive values attached to them: they are incurred not merely for their contributions to productivity (if any) but, in addition, for the manner in which they enhance the individual and collective objectives of managers." [24] He concluded that there is "serious question as to whether studies of monopoly power based on reported profit provide an accurate estimate of the effects of monopoly. It is possible that a nonnegligible part of true monopoly profit is absorbed internally." [25] An association between concentration and various types of increased expenditures does not, of course, mean that a positive relationship would not be expected or found between concentration and reported profits. It does mean, however, that any such relationship

---

sample of data—male operatives and kindred workers in unregulated industries—he observed that "concentration seems to raise earnings by about 33 percent when unions are weak, but by only 13 percent when they are strong" (pp. 104–105). For these same workers, the interaction between concentration and unionism "most commonly has a negative effect" on earnings. Weiss believes that these results "give support to the notion that it is unionism or the threat of unionism that produces high wages in concentrated industries" (pp. 114–115).

[24] Oliver E. Williamson, *The Economics of Discretionary Behavior* (Englewood Cliffs: Prentice-Hall, Inc., 1964), p. 33. See, also, *idem*, "Managerial Discretion and Business Behavior," *American Economic Review*, Vol. LIII, No. 5 (December, 1963), pp. 1032–1057.

[25] *Idem, The Economics . . .* , p. 173.

would be weak or biased downward compared to the true impact of concentration on the total of monopoly rents in all forms.

Finally, concentration may influence the firm's desire to maximize profits. As Scitovsky has pointed out, "when restraints on or costs of entry to a monopolistic or oligopolistic market suspend the operation of the competitive forces that would tend to eliminate profits, then the failure to maximize profit may lead merely to lower-than-maximum profits instead of to the punishment of losses."[26] To the extent that this occurs, we may expect to find a reduced tendency for profits and price-cost margins to be positively related to concentration.

Granting all the problems involved in the realistic classification of data and the accurate measurement of concentration, revenues, and costs, and the still greater problems encountered in drawing valid inferences from the empirical relationships observed, we have nevertheless chosen to examine our hypothesis by means of a large-scale, cross-sectional analysis. Our decision to do so was reinforced by the following comment of Bain:

> There is thus a strong case, in the present state of investigation and knowledge, for eschewing the easy road of presenting a few isolated case studies and encouraging facile and unsupported generalizations from them. Instead, we may find it scientifically more satisfying to emphasize the cross-sectional analysis of certain basic dimensions of performance in numerous industries, striking directly at the goal of valid generalization, even though the dimensions of performance considered must be very few in number and though a great deal of the unique and sometimes important detail concerning individual industries is neglected in the process.[27]

---

[26] Scitovsky, *op. cit.*, pp. 106–107.
[27] Bain, *Industrial Organization*, p. 342.

II
Results of Previous Studies

The large body of literature dealing with concentration measurement and problems of oligopoly and monopoly contains relatively few examples of systematic analysis of empirical indicators of structure and performance on a cross-sectional basis. In this chapter, we summarize the principal findings of previous studies of the concentration-profitability relationship as a background for the report of our own work and a guide to the interpretation of our results.

BAIN

The major study most closely paralleling our approach is that reported in a 1951 article by Bain.[1] This paper presents a full statement of the hypothesis that concentration and profit measures are positively associated and gives the results of a statistical analysis of this association for the period 1936–1940. The analysis covers forty-two (out of 340) manufacturing industries identified by the Census in 1935. The sample industries were all those with "national" markets, high degrees of industry specialization and balanced intra-industry product diversification among the constituent firms, and profit data for three or more major firms available through the Securities and Exchange Commission. Profit data for a total of 335 firms were used in the analysis; in

---

[1] Bain, "Relation of Profit Rate . . . ," pp. 293–324. *Idem,* "Corrigendum," *Quarterly Journal of Economics,* Vol. LXV, No. 4 (November, 1951), p. 602.

about half of the industries, the number of firms for which profit data were available was five or less. The particular profit measure used was "the ratio of annual net profit after income taxes to net worth as of the beginning of the year." This ratio was computed for each firm in each year; then a weighted (by net worth) annual average industry profit rate was computed from the firm data for each industry; and finally a simple average of these annual rates was computed. The association of this last statistic, referred to as "industry average profit rate (1936–40)," with a concentration index showing the share of the eight largest firms in total value of industry output in 1935, was the focus of Bain's analysis. His data are reproduced in table 1, and plotted in figure 1. According to Bain, these data revealed:

> . . . no conclusive indication of any closely observed linear relationship of industry concentration to profit rates. . . . A regression line fitted to the data shows a decided downward slope for profit rates as concentration decreases, but the correlation is poor ($r = .33$). . . . The general showing is that of a fairly high average level of profit rates down to the 70 per cent concentration line, a much lower average level down to the 30 per cent line, and (based on a very small sample) a higher level again below the 30 per cent line . . . The positive conclusion which does emerge is that there is a rather distinct break in average profit-rate showing at the 70 per cent concentration line, and that there is a significant difference in the average of industry average profit rates above and below this line.[2]

This rough dichotomy between "concentrated" and "other" industries was reportedly confirmed in the analysis of average profit rates for individual firms and was not undermined by an examination of other "potential determinants or co-determinants of the profit rate" such as capital structure or cost structure.

---

[2] *Idem*, "Relation of Profit Rate . . . ," pp. 313–314.

TABLE 1   1935 CONCENTRATION RATIOS AND 1936–1940 AVERAGE PROFIT RATES FOR A SAMPLE OF FORTY-TWO INDUSTRIES

Census number	Industry designation	Proportion of value product supplied by eight largest firms (1935)	1936–1940 industry average profit rate after income taxes (percent) [1]
222	Asphalt-felt-base floor covering; linoleum	100.0	9.0
1652	Cigarettes	99.4	14.4
1314	Typewriters and parts	99.3	15.8
108	Chewing gum	97.3	16.9
113	Corn syrup, sugar, oil, and starch	95.0	9.3
1408	Motor vehicles	92.4	16.3
803	Rubber tires and tubes	90.4	8.2
629	Rayon and allied products	90.2	12.1
1301	Agricultural implements	87.7	9.1
1022	Gypsum products	86.4	10.1
1123	Tin cans and other tinware	85.6	9.1
1636	Photographic apparatus and materials	84.9	12.9
1647	Tobacco, chewing and smoking	84.3	11.7
1405	Cars, railroad	84.0	2.8
1201	Aluminum products	83.7	9.7
631	Soap	83.1	15.2
1634	Pens, fountain, etc.	82.8	12.3
1218	Smelting and refining, zinc	82.2	4.7
1315	Washing machines	79.7	14.0
1401	Aircraft and parts	72.8	20.8
133	Liquors, distilled	71.4	14.2
1638	Roofing	68.2	7.4
201	Carpets and rugs	68.2	4.7

TABLE 1 (CONTINUED)

Census number	Industry designation	Proportion of value product supplied by eight largest firms (1935)	1936–1940 industry average profit rate after income taxes (percent) [1]
1112	Steel works and rolling mills	63.8	4.9
123	Meat packing	63.5	3.6
1102	Cast iron pipe	63.0	8.6
705	Petroleum refining	58.9	6.8
1126	Wire	54.0	7.5
115	Flavoring extracts	54.0	1.8
1608	Cigars	50.7	6.9
1104	Doors and shutters, metal	49.0	18.3
1325	Printer's machinery	47.4	2.2
1002	Cement	44.7	5.4
116	Flour	37.0	7.6
907	Leather	34.3	0.8
1117	Screw machine products	32.9	8.2
904	Boots and shoes	30.8	7.5
105	Canned fruits and vegetables	30.4	7.4
209	Rayon manufactures	27.1	8.4
408	Paper goods	23.7	12.4
112	Confectionery	19.9	17.0
311	Lumber and timber products	7.6	9.1

[1] Net profit after income taxes as a percentage of net worth.
SOURCE: Joe S. Bain, "Relation of Profit Rate to Industry Concentration: American Manufacturing, 1936–1940," Quarterly Journal of Economics, Vol. LXV, No. 3 (August, 1951), Table 1, p. 312.

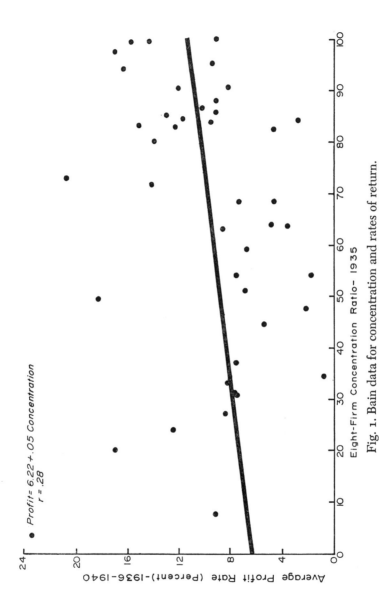

Fig. 1. Bain data for concentration and rates of return.

Our own computations from Bain's data yield a slightly lower correlation value ($r = .28$), and this result is significant only at the 10 percent level. However, the difference in the average profit rate of 11.8 percent for industries with eight-firm concentration of more than 70 percent, and 7.5 percent for industries below this level, is significant at the 2 percent level. Even if Industry 1401, aircraft and parts, the highest profit industry in the sample and one just above the 70 percent concentration line, is excluded from the comparison, the difference between the two groupings remains significant at the 5 percent level.

LEVINSON

As part of a larger study of wage and price movements in manufacturing industry, Levinson [3] analyzed the association between concentration and profits in nineteen major industry groups for the fiscal years 1947–1948 through 1957–1958. The computation of concentration indexes for the analysis from the 1954 data for four-digit industries was described as follows:

> In arriving at the ratios used, the total values of product shipments in each 4-digit industry (within the given 2-digit classification) showing a 50 percent or more concentration ratio for the eight largest companies constituted the numerator. The denominator represented the total value of product shipments for the entire 2-digit industry. The resulting concentration ratios, therefore, reflect the proportion of the total value of product shipments in each 2-digit group represented by "concentrated" 4-digit industries (those in which the eight largest firms accounted for 50 percent or more of the total value of product shipments in 1954) in that group. [4]

---

[3] Harold M. Levinson, *Postwar Movement of Prices and Wages in Manufacturing Industries*, Study Paper No. 21, U.S. Congress, Joint Economic Committee (Washington, January, 1960).

[4] *Ibid.*, p. 26.

TABLE 2   1954 Concentration Indexes, Rates of Return, and Profit Indexes

SIC 2-digit industry group	1954 concentration ratio index	Rates of return on stockholders' equity (percent)				1954 index of profits	Average 1952–1956 index of profits
		1954		Average 1952–1956			
		Before taxes	After taxes	Before taxes	After taxes		
20 Food	22.4	16.8	8.1	17.8	8.4	89.2	92.3
21 Tobacco	100.0	20.9	9.9	22.1	9.9	118.3	121.7
22 Textile mill	11.9	5.3	1.6	9.5	4.0	39.1	51.5
23 Apparel	5.7	10.3	4.4	12.7	5.7	77.6	86.4
24 Lumber	1.5	13.1	7.1	16.5	9.2	71.6	77.8
25 Furniture and fixtures	7.3	15.1	6.7	20.6	9.5	71.9	82.8
26 Paper	5.0	19.8	9.9	22.1	10.7	94.3	98.1
27 Printing and publishing	2.3	20.2	11.5	22.2	12.1	94.7	99.2
28 Chemicals	59.4	22.4	11.7	25.3	12.4	115.6	122.1
29 Petroleum refining	99.1	15.0	12.2	16.5	12.9	95.2	98.0
30 Rubber	51.2	20.6	10.5	24.7	11.4	107.1	112.6
31 Leather	2.3	15.4	8.7	16.3	9.0	113.9	113.1
32 Stone, clay, glass	57.9	23.0	12.2	25.9	12.9	111.5	117.6
33 Primary metals	81.1	16.5	8.8	22.4	11.3	110.0	115.4
34 Fabricated metals	19.3	16.4	7.9	20.6	9.9	72.5	78.1
35 Machinery, nonelectrical	31.1	18.7	8.9	23.6	10.7	89.7	98.9
36 Electrical machinery	72.0	23.6	11.7	27.2	11.9	93.5	97.9
37 Transportation equipment	83.2	30.4	14.6	35.0	15.1	93.9	102.9
38 Instruments	69.9	23.3	11.0	25.0	10.9	n.a.	n.a.
r^2—concentration against each profit variable	—	.289 [b]	.371 [a]	.272 [b]	.339 [b]	.280 [b]	.310 [b]

[a] Significant at 1 percent level.   [b] Significant at 5 percent evel.
SOURCE: Harold M. Levinson, *Postwar Movement of Prices and Wages in Manufacturing Industries*, Study Paper No. 21 (Appendix A), U.S. Congress, Joint Economic Committee (Washington, January, 1960).

TABLE 3   CROSS-SECTION CORRELATION COEFFICIENTS BETWEEN
CONCENTRATION RATIOS AND PROFITS, NINETEEN MANUFACTURING
INDUSTRIES, 1947–1958

Year	Profits before taxes	Profits after taxes
1947–48	−.11	.07
1948–49	.45 c	.53 b
1949–50	.31	.34
1950–51	.36	.37
1951–52	.46 b	.46 b
1952–53	.56 b	.54 b
1953–54	.55 b	.60 a
1954–55	.45 c	.46 b
1955–56	.51 b	.60 a
1956–57	.61 a	.76 a
1957–58	.51 b	.70 a

a Significant at 1 percent level.
b Significant at 5 percent level.
c Significant at 10 percent level.
SOURCE: Harold M. Levinson, *Postwar Movement of Prices and Wages in Manufacturing Industries*, Study Paper No. 21, U.S. Congress, Joint Economic Committee (Washington, January, 1960), p. 3.

The resulting indexes are shown in table 2, along with a selection of profit data from Levinson's tabulations of Federal Trade Commission and Securities and Exchange Commission (FTC-SEC) data. Levinson computed correlation coefficients between his 1954 concentration indexes and rates of return before and after taxes on a cross-sectional basis for each fiscal year covered by his study; the results of these computations are shown in table 3. He concluded that ". . . the data indicate a strong interrelationship, particularly after 1951, between . . . profit levels, and 1954 concentration ratios." [5] Indeed, all the simple correlations between his concentration and profits indexes for 1951–1952 and the following years are significantly different from zero; coefficients for concentration and after-tax profits are significant at the 1 percent level for 1953–1954 and the three fiscal

_____

[5] *Ibid.*, p. 3.

periods 1955–1958. Levinson's results were replicated by us from his data for 1954, and we obtained substantially the same values when the 1954 concentration was correlated with a four-year average of profit rates, 1952–1956 (see table 2).

Levinson also computed, but did not utilize, an "index of profits plus depreciation plus depletion per dollar of sales" from the basic FTC-SEC data; this index is shown in the last two columns of table 2. Correlations of these values with his concentration indexes yield coefficients of .53 ($r^2 = .28$) for the 1954 data and .56 ($r^2 = .31$) for the four-year average. Thus his basic finding of a strong association between concentration and profits on equity is reflected in an association between concentration and a more broadly defined profits-sales relationship. Levinson's data for concentration, after tax rates of return, and the index of profits are plotted in figures 2 and 3.

FUCHS

The study reported by Fuchs [6] focused on the importance of large multi-unit, multi-industry companies in manufacturing industry in 1954. He offered the hypothesis that "the percent of value added accounted for by multi-unit establishments does reflect the ease or difficulty of entry . . . [and therefore] . . . we should be able to use it to predict concentration of ownership and industry rates of profit." [7] He matched thirty-eight (out of 77) roughly three-digit industries with Stigler's data for concentration (1954) and rates of return after taxes on corporate assets (1953–54), and obtained a strong correlation between these concentration indexes and the share of the establishments of multi-

---

[6] Victor Fuchs, "Integration, Concentration, and Profits in Manufacturing Industries," *Quarterly Journal of Economics,* Vol. LXXV, No. 2 (May, 1961), pp. 278–291.
[7] *Ibid.,* p. 285.

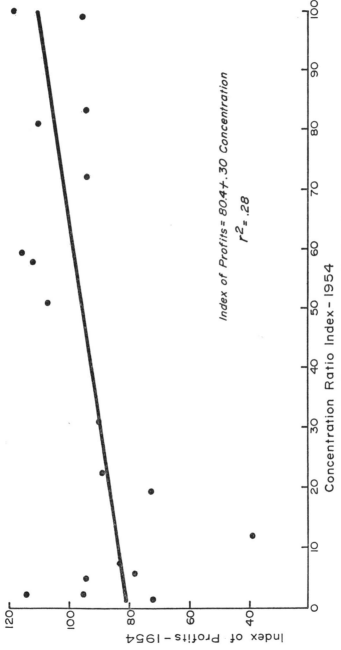

Index of Profits = 80.4+.30 Concentration

$r^2 = .28$

Concentration Ratio Index - 1954

Fig. 2. Levinson data for concentration and index of profits, 1954.

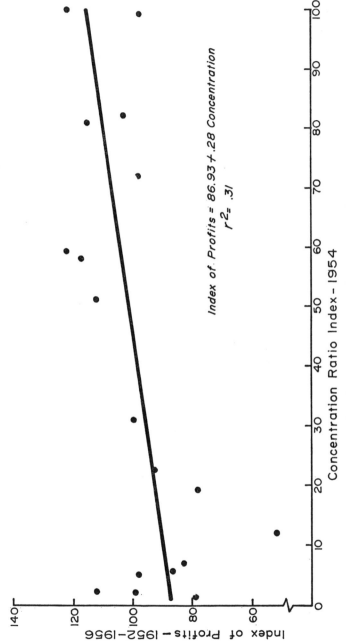

Fig. 3. Levinson data for concentration and index of profits, 1952–1956.

establishment companies in total industry output ($r = .80$). For the concentration and profit measures for the thirty-eight industries, the correlation coefficient is .28, significant at the 10 percent level. In order to see whether the latter result was influenced by the difference between regional and national markets, Fuchs computed a "coefficient of scatter . . . the number of states required to account for 75 percent of industry value added."[8] Taking this coefficient into account as a third variable, he found the partial correlation between profits and concentration in the thirty-eight industries to be .42 and the multiple correlation coefficient to be .49.

WEISS

The analysis of the 1954 concentration data reported by Weiss[9] was conducted at roughly the same level of aggregation as the Levinson study, but the procedures differed substantially. Weiss computed concentration indexes for nineteen two-digit manufacturing industries as weighted averages of selected four-digit *product* concentration ratios within each two-digit group. A system of "adjusted value added" weights was used, although a comparison of weighting systems showed the results to be relatively insensitive to the method employed. Additional adjustments in the average ratios were made "for over- and under-aggregation, and for local and regional markets." The resulting concentration indexes are shown in table 4.

Weiss computed correlation and regression coefficients between these concentration indexes and "average annual rates of return after tax on equity for 40 quarters, 1949–58," obtained from FTC-SEC data. The resulting correlation coefficient, .73, based on twenty-two observations (the Pri-

---

[8] *Ibid.*, p. 287.
[9] Weiss, "Average Concentration Ratios and Industrial Performance," *Journal of Industrial Economics*, Vol. XI, No. 3 (July, 1963), pp. 237–254.

TABLE 4   AVERAGE FOUR-FIRM PRODUCT CONCENTRATION RATIOS
IN TWO-DIGIT CENSUS INDUSTRY GROUPS, 1954

SIC industry group	Number of 4-digit products included	Adjusted average concentration ratio
20 Food and kindred products	42	41.5
21 Tobacco products	4	67.5
22 Textile mill products	29	27.0
23 Apparel and related products	40	14.1
24 Lumber and products	18	15.4
25 Furniture and fixtures	15	17.2
26 Pulp and paper	12	37.4
27 Printing and publishing	16	30.9
28 Chemicals and allied products	39	51.2
29 Petroleum and coal products	6	58.9
30 Rubber products	4	54.8
31 Leather and products	12	28.6
32 Stone, clay and glass	26	52.2
33 Primary metals	20	61.3
34 Fabricated metals	26	37.5
35 Nonelectrical machinery	41	37.7
36 Electrical machinery	21	50.6
37 Transportation equipment	14	60.9
38 Instruments	10	54.1
39 Miscellaneous	38	23.7

SOURCE: Leonard W. Weiss, "Average Concentration Ratios and Industrial
Performance," *Journal of Industrial Economics*, Vol. XI, No. 3 (July,
1963), Tables I and II, p. 239 and p. 242.

mary Metal and Transportation Equipment industry groups
were subdivided for purposes of this computation), is highly
significant. When output growth was introduced as an additional variable the correlation was increased to .84
($R^2 = .69$). Weiss summarized his entire collection of results
by noting that they "re-enforce other empirical findings that
had sometimes been made quite tentatively. In general they
support the traditional views about the impact of concentration on resource allocation and distribution . . ." [10]

---

[10] *Ibid.*, p. 253.

SCHWARTZMAN

Schwartzman [11] presents an example of a cross-sectional analysis relating concentration to the current price-cost ratio. His major interest was in measuring the difference in the ratio of average variable cost to price (P/AVC) between monopolistic and competitive industries. His two hypotheses are: "(1) the ratio of price to average variable cost is higher in monopolistic than in competitive industries; (2) among monopolistic industries, the ratio of price to average variable cost declines with the degree of monopoly." [12] He discriminates between monopolistic and competitive industries according to whether the four largest firms account for 50 percent or more of total employment; the degree of monopoly is equated with the four-firm employment concentration ratio. His measure of the price-cost relationship is the ratio

---

[11] David Schwartzman, "The Effect of Monopoly on Price," *Journal of Political Economy*, Vol. LXVII, No. 4 (August, 1959), pp. 352–362. Sato also explored the effect of concentration in a general study of price-cost structure. Net margin before taxes as a percentage of sales was the dependent variable, and the explanatory variables included the four-firm concentration level, capital-sales ratio, and a measure of regional-local markets. Two industry samples were used, derived from *Statistics of Income* data. Concentration indexes were grouped into three categories: high (50 and above), medium (30 to 49), and low (under 30). Using concentration data for 1954 and income data for 1948–1956, Sato concluded:

"For the 54-industry sample we found that the high concentration group had a significantly positive effect on percentage net margins, but the moderate concentration group did not. . . . However, with the larger sample [110 industries] statistical evidence is not so clear in this respect. . . . We can probably state as a rough estimate that the high concentration group charged, on the average, percentage net margins 2 to 3 percentage points higher than the competitive level. . . . In contrast, the moderate concentration group did not have any significant influence on price-cost gaps as compared with the low concentration group" (p. 403). The mean margin for the entire industry sample was 7 percent. Kazuo Sato, "Price-Cost Structure and Behavior of Profit Margins," *Yale Economic Essays*, Vol. 1, No. 2 (Fall, 1961), pp. 361–418.

[12] Schwartzman, *op. cit.*, p. 354.

of "gross value product to direct cost," the latter including "costs of materials, fuel, purchased electricity, and production workers' wages." The arbitrary elements and biases introduced in these computations are fully recognized.

The second innovation in Schwartzman's study is his use of a comparison of United States and Canadian industries as the focus of analysis rather than a direct observation of the concentration and profit relationship within United States industries. Using the criterion of 50 percent of total employment in four firms, Schwartzman classifies pairs of four-digit industries for the two countries as to whether the members of each pair are (*a*) both concentrated, (*b*) both unconcentrated, or (*c*) mixed. He then computes the ratios of revenue to direct cost for each member of each pair, and then the ratio between the two ratios. Taking unweighted averages of these relative profit indexes, he obtains the following results:

> For 27 unconcentrated pairs, the average P/AVC ratio (Canada/U.S.) is 101.9.
> For 15 concentrated pairs, the average P/AVC ratio (more concentrated–less concentrated) is 104.8.
> For 19 mixed pairs, the average P/AVC ratio (concentrated-unconcentrated) is 107.1.

The last two groupings are further broken down according to (*a*) purely domestic industries, (*b*) industries competing with imports, and (*c*) export industries. When these finer results for the mixed pairs are compared with the basic ratio between Canada and the United States (101.9), significant differences are observed for all industries except those involving export trade. Schwartzman concludes that "monopolistic industries, other than those which have a large export trade, have higher P/AVC ratios than do competitive industries." [13] However, a similar analysis among the concentrated

---

[13] *Ibid.*, p. 359.

pairs does not reveal a significant difference. Thus he observes that "both Bain's and the present study fail to confirm the belief that the degree of monopoly, defined in terms of concentration ratios, is a continuous function of the monopoly effect on price." [14]

We have rearranged Schwartzman's data and computed correlations between the concentration index and P/AVC ratio by industry for the three comparable groups of industries. Our results are as follows:

	Number of Industries	r^2
U.S. industries, 4-firm CR	61	.094 [b]
Canadian industries, 4-firm CR	32	.088 [c]
Canadian industries, 3-firm CR	29	.072

[b] Significant at 5 percent level.
[c] Significant at 10 percent level.

Evidently the association between relative concentration and margin levels is not strongly reflected in the direct analysis of the data, although the correlation result for United States industries is significant at the 5 percent level. However, when the Schwartzman data are grouped by deciles, as in table 5, a rough association between concentration and the average levels of the P/AVC ratio is observed. As in Bain's data, the 70 percent concentration level (for three or four firms in this instance, rather than eight) proves a convenient breaking point. In each of the three sets of data, the differences in the average P/AVC index for industries below and above 70 percent concentration are statistically significant.

[14] *Ibid.*, p. 361.

TABLE 5   FREQUENCY DISTRIBUTION AND AVERAGE P/AVC RATIO FOR
U.S. AND CANADIAN INDUSTRIES, BY CONCENTRATION DECILES, 1954

Concentration decile	Number of industries	Average P/AVC ratio
United States, 4-firm CR		
0.00– 9.99	2	125.3
10.00– 19.99	14	130.0
20.00– 29.99	9	132.1
30.00– 39.99	7	153.8
40.00– 49.99	14	138.0
50.00– 59.99	7	138.2
60.00– 69.99	3	129.9
70.00– 79.99	4	169.2
80.00– 89.99	1	176.4
90.00–100.00	0	—
Average: below 70	56	136.1
70 and above	5	170.6
Canada, 3-firm CR		
0.00– 9.99	4	133.5
10.00– 19.99	4	130.3
20.00– 29.99	0	—
30.00– 39.99	4	137.0
40.00– 49.99	1	151.5
50.00– 59.99	3	124.5
60.00– 69.99	5	140.4
70.00– 79.99	2	124.4
80.00– 89.99	3	138.9
90.00–100.00	3	161.2
Average: below 70	21	134.8
70 and above	8	143.6
Canada, 4-firm CR		
0.00– 9.99	1	126.6
10.00– 19.99	2	132.7
20.00– 29.99	3	165.4
30.00– 39.99	4	136.8
40.00– 49.99	5	129.7
50.00– 59.99	2	164.2
60.00– 69.99	5	151.5
70.00– 79.99	4	147.0
80.00– 89.99	3	213.4
90.00–100.00	3	144.9
Average: below 70	22	144.1
70 and above	10	166.3

SOURCE: David Schwartzman, "The Effect of Monopoly on Price," *Journal of Political Economy*, Vol. LXVII, No. 4 (August, 1959), Tables 1–3, pp. 358–360.

STIGLER

As part of his comprehensive investigation of the return to capital in manufacturing industries, Stigler [15] analyzed the association between concentration levels and rates of return. His basic data for capital and rates of return are tabulated on a three-digit industry basis as used by the Internal Revenue Service. He then computed weighted averages of the four-firm shipments concentration ratios for the four- or five-digit product classes within each three-digit industry. These weighted average three-digit industry concentration ratios were obtained for 1935, 1947, and 1954. Results for each industry for each pair of years were averaged in order to produce estimates of average industry concentration for each of the two periods covered by the study, 1938–1947 and 1947–1956. The industries for which data are available were then classified as (a) concentrated, (b) unconcentrated, or (c) ambiguous, according to the following criterion:

Concentrated: Only industries classified as having national markets, and the four largest firms account for more than 60 percent of shipments.
Unconcentrated: Either (1) industries classified as having national markets and the four largest firms account for less than 50 percent of shipments; or (2) industries classified as having regional markets, and the four largest firms account for less than 20 percent of shipments.
Ambiguous: All other industries.[16]

Professor Stigler has kindly made available a more detailed tabulation of his data than that published in his own

---

[15] Stigler, *Capital and Rates of Return* . . .
[16] The following industries that would have been classified as unconcentrated by these criteria were assigned to the ambiguous category because of their internal heterogeneity: miscellaneous foods, miscellaneous apparel, miscellaneous rubber goods, miscellaneous stone products, and manufacturing, nec.

study, and his list of 98 industries classified by geographic scope of market is reproduced in Appendix B, along with selected data used in our own subsequent analysis.

Stigler's own results are summarized in table 6. He de-

TABLE 6   Average Rate of Return on Assets in Concentrated, Unconcentrated, and Ambiguous Industries, 1938–1957

	Industries [1]		
	Concentrated	Unconcentrated	Ambiguous
Number of industries	14	54	31
Period	Average rate of return (percent)		
1938–41	6.51	5.25	6.59
1942–44	6.23	7.68	7.19
1945–47	7.30	10.01	8.64
1948–50	9.11	8.02	8.90
1951–54	6.33	5.05	5.90
1955–57	7.05	5.44	6.35

[1] The aircraft and parts industry was included in this computation but excluded from subsequent analysis and the summary tables. Hence the total of 99 industries here.

Source: George J. Stigler, *Capital and Rates of Return in Manufacturing Industries* (Princeton: Princeton University Press, 1963), Table 17, p. 68.

scribes them as "somewhat ambiguous, but on the whole . . . negative." Although the concentrated industries have higher average rates of return in 1938–1941 and after 1948, and the difference between concentrated and unconcentrated industries is statistically significant at the 5 percent and 2 percent levels in 1951–1954 and 1955–1957, respectively, there is only a slight difference for longer periods, and an adjustment for the withdrawals of officers of small corporations would cause the differences to "almost vanish." [17] The weakness of these results was confirmed by correlation analysis. When the industries were separated into those with national, regional, and local markets, simple

[17] Stigler, *Capital and Rates of Return* . . . , pp. 67–68.

correlation results between average concentration ratios for the years 1947–1954 and average rates of return (corrected for officers' withdrawals) for the same years were not significantly different from zero at the 10 percent level.[18] Stigler points out that the absence of an affirmative finding may be due to the higher value of assets in concentrated industries, reflecting the capitalized value of the stream of monopoly returns. This "untestable" interpretation is questioned, however, because of the large variance in the rates of return among concentrated industries.

Our secondary analysis of Stigler's data yielded substantially similar results. We retained his classification of industries according to the geographic scope of their markets, but reclassified the national-market industries separately for 1947 and 1954 as concentrated, unconcentrated, or ambiguous according to his criteria, with the exceptions listed in note 16, above. From Stigler's rate-of-return data, we selected the individual years 1947 and 1954 and averages for 1947–1948 and 1953–1955. (Only about half of the 1946 rates of return could be matched to the 1947 industry classifications; hence a three-year centered average for the earlier period was not feasible.)

Mean rates of return for national-market industries classified as concentrated, unconcentrated, and ambiguous in each year are compared in table 7. The concentrated industries show lower rates of return in the earlier period, although the differences are not statistically significant. In both of the later-period comparisons (1954 alone and 1953–55) the concentrated industries show higher rates of return, and the differences between concentrated and unconcentrated industries are significant at the 1 percent level.

---

[18] The correlation coefficients reported were as follows: seventy-five national market industries, .13; fourteen regional market industries, −.085; nine local market industries, −.379; *ibid.*, pp. 68–69. The number of national market industries was erroneously given as twenty-five; this error was corrected in correspondence.

TABLE 7 AVERAGE RATES OF RETURN ON ASSETS FOR CONCENTRATED, UNCONCENTRATED, AND AMBIGUOUS NATIONAL INDUSTRIES, AND STATISTICAL SIGNIFICANCE TESTS [1]

	Number of industries	Average rate of return on assets (percent)	t Ratios for differences between means		
			Concentrated-ambiguous	Concentrated-unconcentrated	Ambiguous-unconcentrated
1947 [2]			.14	.73	.34
Concentrated	14	9.64			
Ambiguous	6	9.87			
Unconcentrated	55	10.42			
1947–48 average [2]			.43	.61	.08
Concentrated	14	9.22			
Ambiguous	6	9.83			
Unconcentrated	55	9.72			
1954 [3]			1.69	2.76 [a]	.19
Concentrated	14	6.01			
Ambiguous	7	4.19			
Unconcentrated	54	4.38			
1953–55 average [3]			2.20 [b]	2.86 [a]	.37
Concentrated	14	6.60			
Ambiguous	7	4.64			
Unconcentrated	54	4.94			

[1] Definitions based on 4-firm concentration ratios, as follows: concentrated, > 60 percent; ambiguous, 50–59.9 percent; unconcentrated, < 50 percent. [3] Data grouped by 1954 concentration ratio.
[2] Data grouped by 1947 concentration ratio. [b] Significant at 5 percent level.
[a] Significant at 1 percent level.
SOURCE: Computed from George J. Stigler, *Capital and Rates of Return in Manufacturing Industries* (Princeton: Princeton University Press, 1963), and supplementary information supplied by Professor Stigler in correspondence (Appendix B).

A correlation analysis was made for all ninety-eight industries grouped according to the geographic scope of their
markets and using each of the rate-of-return series in Appendix B. The results of this analysis are shown in table 8. Only
the results for the seventy-five industries with national mar-

TABLE 8   REGRESSION RESULTS FOR CONCENTRATION AND RATES OF
RETURN, BY GEOGRAPHIC SCOPE OF MARKETS

| Scope of market | Number of industries | Period of comparison for: | | Regression coefficient for concentration variable | r^2 |
		Concentration	Rate of return		
National	75	1947	1947	−.023	.011
		1947	1947–48	−.008	.002
		1954	1954	.043 [a]	.132
		1954	1953–55	.044 [a]	.154
Regional	14	1947	1947	−.055	.045
		1947	1947–48	−.037	.026
		1954	1954	.042	.043
		1954	1953–55	.056	.124
Local	9	1947	1947	−.048	.043
		1947	1947–48	−.027	.014
		1954	1954	.013	.052
		1954	1953–55	−.002	.003

[a] Significant at 1 percent level.
SOURCE: Computed from Stigler data (see Appendix B).

kets in the later period are statistically significant. The
regression coefficients, although small, are significant at the
1 percent level, and the correlation coefficients are similar to
those obtained in other studies. The scatter of the data and
the fitted regression line are shown in figure 4.

The ambiguity of Stigler's findings in this study is increased by the results of a later investigation [19] in which he

[19] *Idem,* "A Theory of Oligopoly." The conflict between Stigler's results
has been commented upon by Richard B. Heflebower also; see U.S. Congress, Senate, Subcommittee on Antitrust and Monopoly, Committee on the
Judiciary, *Hearings, Economic Concentration,* 88th Cong., 2d Sess., 1964,
"Part 2. Mergers and other Factors Affecting Industry Concentration,"
pp. 777–807.

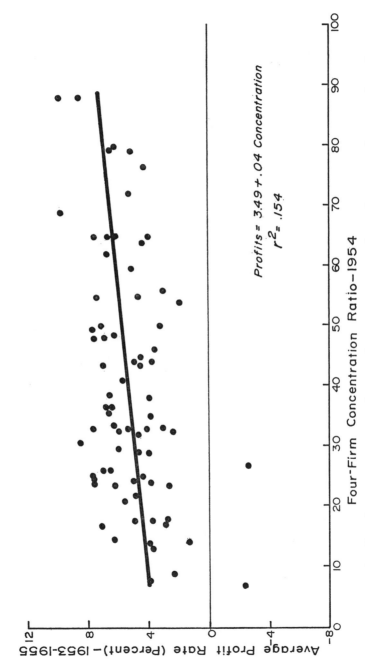

Fig. 4. Stigler data for concentration and rates of return in seventy-five industries with national markets.

found a positive association between concentration and profits in a sample of seventeen manufacturing industries for which profit data were available for large firms accounting for an important share of total sales. Stigler's data for four-

TABLE 9 PROFITABILITY AND CONCENTRATION DATA, SEVENTEEN INDUSTRIES

Industry [1]	4-firm concentra- tion, 1954	Average rate of return (percent), 1953–1957	
		All assets	Net worth
Sulphur mining (4)	98	19.03	23.85
Automobiles (3)	98	11.71	20.26
Flat glass (3)	90	11.79	16.17
Gypsum products (2)	90	12.16	20.26
Primary aluminum (4)	98	6.87	13.46
Metal cans (4)	80	7.27	13.90
Chewing gum (2)	86	13.50	17.06
Hard-surface floor coverings (3)	87	6.56	7.59
Cigarettes (5)	83	7.23	11.18
Industrial gases (3)	84	8.25	11.53
Corn wet milling (3)	75	9.17	11.55
Typewriters (3)	83	3.55	5.39
Domestic laundry equipment (2)	68	9.97	17.76
Rubber tires (9)	79	7.86	14.02
Rayon fiber (4)	76	5.64	6.62
Carbon black (2)	73	8.29	9.97
Distilled liquors (6)	64	6.94	7.55
Correlation results:			
Rank correlation with concentration index		.32	.51
Linear correlation (r) with concentration index		.46 [c]	.53 [b]

[1] The number of firms is given in parentheses after the industry title. Only those industries are included for which a substantial share (35 percent or more) of the industry's sales is accounted for by the firms in the sample; these firms derive their chief revenues (50 percent or more) from the industry. Additional explanation of the original table is as follows: "The rates of return are weighted averages for the numbers of firms given in parentheses; the income data are taken from Moody's Manuals and the concept employed is net income after taxes but before interest paid. The Herfindahl indexes include very rough estimates of the shares of other companies in the industry but, by their nature, primarily reflect the shares of the top companies." Letter from Claire Friedland, November 16, 1965.
[b] Significant at 5 percent level.   [c] Significant at 10 percent level.
SOURCE: George J. Stigler, "A Theory of Oligopoly," *Journal of Political Economy*, Vol. LXXII, No. 1 (February, 1964), Table 7, p. 58.

firm concentration and average rates of return (after taxes) on assets and net worth for the seventeen industries are shown in table 9, along with correlation coefficients computed from them. Stigler's own analysis was based upon the rank correlation coefficients between industry rate of return and both the four-firm concentration index and H, the Herfindahl (sum of squared percentages) index of concentration. We have also computed linear correlation coefficients, as shown in the table. Stigler comments that "the data suggest that there is no relationship between profitability and concentration if H is less than 0.250 or the share of the 4 largest firms is less than about 80 percent."[20] Our own computations indicate relatively weak relationships, although the correlation between concentration and rate of return on net worth is significant at the 5 percent level. The data are plotted in figure 5, which shows the scatter of points and the anomalous position of the domestic laundry equipment industry (two firms) in the sample.

SHERMAN

In a statistical analysis of the association between corporate profit rates, corporate size, and cyclical stability, Sherman[21] examined the concentration and profits relationship at the two-digit industry level. For twenty major manufacturing industry groups, he computed the weighted average of the component four-digit industry concentration ratios for the eight largest firms in 1954 and the corresponding profit before taxes as a percentage of stockholders' equity. His results are shown in table 10 and plotted in figure 6. The correlation between the two series is .66, significant at the 1 percent level.

---

[20] Stigler, "A Theory of Oligopoly," p. 57.
[21] Sherman, *op. cit.*, Chap. 8.

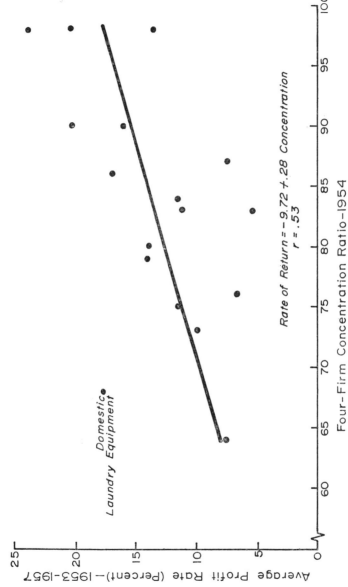

Fig. 5. Concentration and rates of return in seventeen industries, based on Stigler data.

TABLE 10   PROFIT RATES AND CONCENTRATION RATIOS BY INDUSTRY
GROUP, ALL MANUFACTURING CORPORATIONS, 1954

Industry group	8-firm concentration ratio	Rate of return on equity (percent)
Motor vehicles and parts [1]	98.1	27.1
Tobacco	91.5	20.3
Transportation equipment [1]	75.6	29.8
Rubber	74.2	17.8
Primary metal	70.8	13.0
Chemicals	63.3	19.9
Electrical machinery	60.8	20.7
Petroleum and coal	57.7	7.7
Instruments	56.1	23.9
Stone, clay, glass	55.0	19.9
Food and beverages	45.7	14.4
Machinery, except electrical	44.4	16.2
Fabricated metal	40.3	15.6
Paper	39.4	17.3
Textile mill	37.1	5.1
Leather	33.7	11.4
Furniture	23.8	12.8
Printing and publishing	21.5	15.1
Apparel	20.5	7.6
Lumber	15.5	12.2

$r = .66$ (significant at 1 percent level)

[1] The Transportation Equipment industry was divided to present Motor
Vehicles and Parts separately as the weighted average of its own com-
ponents.
SOURCE: Howard J. Sherman, *Macrodynamic Economics* (New York:
Appleton-Century-Crofts, 1964), Table 8-4, p. 143.

SUMMARY OF RESULTS

Selected results of the previous studies of concentration
and profits are summarized in table 11, along with some of
the results of our own secondary analysis. The coefficient of
determination is used as a summary statistic and for direct
comparison with our own findings presented in the following
chapters. Absence of a note indicating the significance level
of the coefficient shows that it is not significantly different
from zero at the 10 percent level.

The studies cover different periods, are based on different

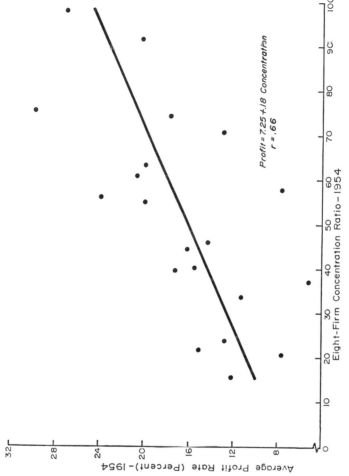

Fig. 6. Concentration and profit rates, 1954, based on Sherman data.

TABLE 11   Concentration-profits Studies, Selected Summary Data

Study	Level of industry classification	Number of firms in concentration ratio	Number of industries or industry groups	Profit measure	Period — Concentration	Period — Profits	Results¹ (r²)
Bain	4-digit	8	42	Rate of return on net worth after taxes	1935	Avg. 1936–40	.109 b [.078 c]
		8	19	Rate of return on equity after taxes	1954	Annual, 1947–58	.005 to .570 a; median = .278 b
Levinson	2-digit	8	18	Profits plus depreciation and depletion as a percentage of sales	1954 / 1954	1954 / Avg. 1952–56	[.371 a / .339 b] [.280 b / .310 b]
Fuchs	3-digit	4	38	Rate of return on assets after taxes	1954	Avg. 1953–54	.081 c
Weiss	2-digit	4	22	Rate of return on equity after taxes	1954	Avg. 1949–58	.533 a
Schwartzman	4-digit	4 (U.S.) / 4 (Canada) / 3 (Canada)	61 / 32 / 29	Gross value of product as a percentage of direct cost	1954	1954	[.094 b / .088 c / .072]

TABLE 11 (CONTINUED)

Study	Level of industry classification	Number of firms in concentration ratio	Number of industries or industry groups	Profit measure	Period		Results [1] (r^2)
					Concentration	Profits	
Stigler (I)	3-digit	4	75	Rate of return on corporate assets after taxes	Avg. 1947–54	Avg. 1947–54	.017
					1947	1947	[.011]
					1947	Avg. 1947–48	[.002]
					1954	1954	[.132 a]
					1954	Avg. 1953–55	[.154 a]
Stigler (II)	4-digit	4	17	Rate of return on assets after taxes	1954	Avg. 1953–57	[.209 c]
				Rate of return on net worth after taxes	1954	Avg. 1953–57	[.283 b]
Sherman	2-digit	8	20	Rate on return on equity after taxes	1954	1954	[.429 a]

[1] Results of our secondary analysis shown in brackets.   [b] Significant at 5 percent level.   [c] Significant at 10 percent level.
[a] Significant at 1 percent level.

levels of industry classification, and use different measures of both concentration and profit variables. In general, it would appear that analysis based upon two-digit industry group classifications yields stronger results than that based on three-digit or four-digit classifications. Some possible reasons for this result will be explored after the presentation of our own findings based on concentration data for 1958 in the following chapters. Analysis of concentration data for 1954 and appropriate rate-of-return series seems to yield stronger results than analysis based on earlier data, although the number of earlier examples is not great.

It is tempting to explain the latter difference in terms of Hultgren's recent findings on the cyclical behavior of margins in manufacturing industries.[22] He found that profits per dollar of sales in manufacturing tended to rise and fall with quantity sold, and that these fluctuations were due more to changes in unit costs than to changes in prices. The period 1947–1948 was one of general economic expansion, whereas the trough of a five-quarter contraction occurred in the middle of 1954. Thus we would expect 1947–1948 to be a period in which margins and profits were rising, and 1953–1954 to be a period in which they were falling, and indeed this appears to be true. Average profit levels relative to both sales and capital were also higher in the earlier period. Hence it may be that the high and rising profits of the expansion period roughly eliminated the profit advantage of the concentrated industries and therefore removed any association between concentration and profits in the 1947 data. By contrast, the contraction in 1953–1954 may have had a sharper effect on profits in the less concentrated industries, thus revealing an association between concentration and profits when data for that period are used.

This cyclical explanation of the disparity in the general results is consistent with a number of other pieces of evi-

---

[22] Hultgren, *op. cit.*

dence. Sherman concluded that "the profit margins of small firms in more competitive industries generally turn down at cycle peaks significantly earlier than the profit margins of larger firms in more concentrated industries." "There is a tendency . . . for the industries with the lowest degree of concentration to have the highest cyclical amplitudes of profit margins." [23] It has also been suggested that managerial "expense preferences" may be more freely exercised during periods of prosperity and curbed during recession. This would contribute to a counter-cyclical stability in the profits of larger firms. The greater cyclical instability of profit records in smaller firms has been frequently noted.[24] An earlier study revealed that the inequality of size among giant firms in the economy as a whole tends to increase during economic contractions because of the slower growth of the smaller giant firms.[25] If the larger giant firms are in the more concentrated industries, the poorer profit experience of the less concentrated industries and the slower growth of their leading firms are associated indicators of the uneven effects of cyclical instability. As a result, concentration levels and profit records would show a stronger association in periods of contraction than in periods of economic expansion. During expansion periods, the smaller firms and less concentrated industries apparently experience growth rates and profits more nearly similar to those of large firms and more concentrated industries.

In almost all the analyses based primarily upon United States concentration data for 1954, a significant although weak association between concentration and profits is observed. The sole exceptions to this statement are our secondary analyses of Stigler's data for fourteen regional and nine

---

[23] Sherman, *op. cit.*, p. 147 and pp. 150–151.
[24] Stigler, *Capital and Rates of Return . . .* , and Stekler, *op. cit.*
[25] Norman R. Collins and Lee E. Preston, "The Size Structure of the Largest Industrial Firms," *American Economic Review*, Vol. LI, No. 5 (December, 1961), pp. 986–1011.

local industries (see table 8). Although the strength and the statistical reliability of these results vary considerably, the finding of significant associations in a substantial number of different samples of data under different statistical treatments strongly suggests an underlying functional relationship. Fortunately, 1958 is cyclically similar to 1954 (a four-quarter general contraction ended in the middle of 1958), and thus data for the two years should be cyclically comparable in some respects. Our analysis of 1958 data in the following chapters is thus a test of the persistence of the concentration-profits associations observed in 1954.

III

Profits and Concentration in Major Industry Groups

Systematic investigation of the concentration-profitability relationship has been impeded by the lack of direct correspondence between the available collections of data for the two variables. The concentration data are available on the four- and five-digit Standard Industrial Classification basis, and even these categories are sometimes criticized as being insufficiently refined. Major collections of profit data are generally tabulated for more highly aggregated industry groups, and even here some inaccuracies arise because of the assignment of consolidated profits of multi-industry companies to their principal industry categories. Thus both sets of data are imperfect, and the two together do not constitute a single series of paired observations. To examine the concentration-profitability relationship, the analyst must either combine the concentration indexes to produce an average value corresponding to the industry classifications for which profit data are tabulated, or else develop, on an *ad hoc* basis, profit indicators for more narrowly defined industry categories.

Our analysis of the concentration data for 1958 involves both procedures. In this chapter we focus on the twenty two-digit major manufacturing industry groups. This analysis makes use of available profit data for these groups and allows us to relate our own profit measure, the percentage margin on sales, to other indicators of profitability. A weighted average index of concentration for the constituent four-digit industries of each group must, however, be used as the concentration variable. In the next chapter, we use the four-digit industry concentration ratios, and analyze in detail the association between them and the percentage price-cost margin. The results reported in this chapter are of intrinsic interest, particularly in comparison with the results of other studies based on two-digit industry group data. This analysis also serves to validate the margin index as a profitability indicator. The subsequent comparison of results from this and the next chapter permits a check of the previous evidence that a stronger concentration-profitability relationship exists among broadly categorized industry aggregates than among more narrowly defined industries.

CONCENTRATION DATA

Our statistical analysis deals entirely with concentration measured in terms of the share of the four largest firms in the total value of shipments accounted for by each four-digit Census manufacturing industry.[1] Averages of the concentration ratios, weighted by value of shipments for each industry, are used to estimate concentration levels for each two-digit major industry group. Industry definitions for the 1958 concentration data follow the amended version of the 1945 *SIC Manual* used in the 1954 Census of Manufactures.[2]

The number of four-digit industries, the range of four-digit industry concentration ratios, and the weighted average index of concentration for each two-digit group are shown in table 12. There are considerable differences among the major groups in the number of four-digit industries included, as well as in the average level and dispersion of the concentration ratios. For example, in the Lumber and Wood

---

[1] Data obtained from U.S. Congress, Senate, Subcommittee on Antitrust and Monopoly, Committee on the Judiciary, *Concentration Ratios.* . . .

[2] For a reconciliation of the two classification systems, see U.S. Bureau of the Census, *U.S. Census of Manufactures: 1958. Vol. 1, Summary Statistics,* 1961, Appendix C.

TABLE 12 AVERAGE 1958 FOUR-FIRM CONCENTRATION RATIOS AND RELATED DATA FOR TWO-DIGIT INDUSTRY GROUPS

	SIC industry group	Number of 4-digit industries	Weighted average concentration	Range of concentration for 4-digit industries
20	Food and kindred products	42	32.38	11–88
21	Tobacco products	4	73.93	54–79
22	Textile mill products	32	29.03	7–83
23	Apparel and related products	41	13.74	3–59
24	Lumber and wood products	18	11.38	7–93
25	Furniture and fixtures	15	18.78	9–58
26	Paper and allied products	12	25.70	17–69
27	Printing and publishing	16	17.69	6–45
28	Chemicals and allied products	41	45.72	18–93
29	Petroleum and coal products	5	31.87	11–63
30	Rubber and plastic products	4	52.20	23–87
31	Leather and leather products	12	24.34	10–70
32	Stone, clay and glass products	29	38.19	4–92
33	Primary metal industries	19	50.02	16–97
34	Fabricated metal products	30	27.25	5–91
35	Machinery, except electrical	41	36.33	7–87
36	Electrical machinery	21	45.03	17–92
37	Transportation equipment	14	62.36	18–97
38	Instruments and related products	10	47.78	28–65
39	Miscellaneous manufacturing	38	22.23	5–81

SOURCE: U.S. Congress, Senate, Subcommittee on Antitrust and Monopoly, Committee on the Judiciary, *Concentration Ratios in Manufacturing Industry, 1958*, Table 2. Averages computed from 4-digit industry data using value of shipments as weights.

Products industry group, the concentration ratio of 11 percent represents an averaging of ratios for the eighteen component four-digit industries ranging from 7 to 93 percent. The narrowest range of ratios (54 to 79 percent) occurs for the Tobacco Products group, which includes only four component four-digit industries.

PROFIT MEASURES

The weighted average 1958 concentration ratios were related to three sets of profit measures, computed for each of the two-digit major industry groups: (1) 1958 profits before and after taxes as a percentage of sales, assets, and shareholders' equity; (2) average 1956–1960 profits before and after taxes as a percentage of sales, assets, and shareholders' equity; and (3) the 1958 price-cost margins.

The first two sets of profit measures are rates-of-return data published by the Federal Trade Commission and the Securities and Exchange Commission in the *Quarterly Financial Report for Manufacturing Corporations.* Quarterly estimates are given in this publication for corporations classified by two-digit major industry groups. These quarterly data have been combined to obtain the 1958 and average 1956–1960 profit rates used in this analysis and are shown in table 13.

The third profit measure, the price-cost margin, has been constructed to provide a basis for the analysis of the concentration-profits relationship at the four-digit industry level, presented in the next chapter. The margin index is essentially the difference between gross revenues and direct costs, expressed as a percentage of the revenues. The figure for the difference was obtained by subtracting payroll and other direct costs from the Census value-added figure for each four-digit industry. The value-added figure is equal to the total value of shipments of products manufactured, plus receipts for services rendered, less the cost of materials, supplies and containers, fuel, purchased electric energy, and

TABLE 13 PROFIT AND PRICE-COST MARGIN DATA FOR TWENTY TWO-DIGIT INDUSTRY GROUPS, 1958 AND AVERAGE 1956–1960

| SIC industry group | 1958 profits | | | | | | Average 1956–1960 profits | | | | | | 1958 Price-cost margin |
| | Before taxes as percent of: | | | After taxes as percent of: | | | Before taxes as percent of: | | | After taxes as percent of: | | | |
	Sales	Assets	Shhldrs. equity	Sales	Assets	Shhldrs. equity	Sales	Assets	Shhldrs. equity	Sales	Assets	Shhldrs. equity	
20 Food	4.48	11.30	17.42	2.24	5.64	8.70	4.70	11.60	18.04	2.32	5.74	8.93	14.50
21 Tobacco	11.20	17.07	28.22	5.35	8.16	13.49	10.96	16.08	26.83	5.26	7.72	12.89	27.33
22 Textile	3.36	5.02	7.39	1.57	2.35	3.46	4.70	7.31	10.86	2.31	3.61	5.36	11.70
23 Apparel	2.25	6.21	11.63	.96	2.64	4.94	2.79	7.64	14.71	1.35	3.69	7.11	14.66
24 Lumber	5.12	6.86	10.46	2.80	3.75	5.72	5.33	7.52	11.52	2.97	4.19	6.42	10.49
25 Furniture and fixtures	4.43	8.93	13.67	2.04	4.11	6.29	5.31	11.12	17.27	2.56	5.38	8.35	16.28
26 Paper	9.26	10.93	15.72	4.74	5.60	8.06	10.17	12.53	18.16	5.21	6.43	9.32	17.64
27 Printing and publishing	6.35	10.81	18.19	3.13	5.33	8.97	7.26	12.67	21.66	3.72	6.50	11.12	23.07
28 Chemicals	12.76	14.44	20.86	6.95	7.87	11.37	14.17	16.66	24.13	7.59	8.92	12.92	31.45
29 Petroleum & coal products	10.06	7.94	10.77	9.26	7.32	9.92	11.56	9.56	13.03	9.98	8.24	11.22	5.63
30 Rubber and plastic	7.15	11.37	18.55	3.50	5.58	9.10	7.78	12.56	20.69	3.95	6.38	10.51	18.73
31 Leather	3.77	7.85	12.72	1.68	3.50	5.66	4.06	8.73	14.57	1.92	4.14	6.92	15.33
32 Stone, clay & glass	12.44	13.62	18.77	6.76	7.40	10.20	13.85	16.23	22.49	7.40	8.66	12.01	24.60
33 Primary metal	9.85	9.09	12.93	5.16	4.76	6.77	11.35	12.15	17.65	5.99	6.41	9.31	14.51
34 Fabricated metal	6.34	10.07	15.07	3.06	4.87	7.28	6.58	10.81	16.55	3.24	5.33	8.16	16.20
35 Machinery, except electrical	7.76	9.42	14.53	3.65	4.44	6.85	9.19	12.23	19.32	4.50	5.99	9.47	17.54
36 Electrical machinery	7.65	12.18	20.42	3.82	6.09	10.22	8.01	13.17	22.76	3.95	6.49	11.22	20.73
37 Transportation equipment	6.21	9.63	16.49	3.34	5.17	8.86	8.54	13.92	24.68	4.24	6.92	12.26	15.08
38 Instruments	11.31	15.03	22.13	5.43	7.22	10.63	11.96	16.22	24.30	5.86	7.96	11.93	23.79
39 Miscellaneous [1]	6.30	10.53	16.95	3.03	5.06	8.15	6.53	11.19	18.56	3.22	5.53	9.18	16.17

[1] Data include ordinance group.

SOURCE: U.S. Federal Trade Commission and U.S. Securities and Exchange Commission, *Quarterly Financial Report for Manufacturing Corporations*, 1956–1960, and Appendix A.

contract work. From value added, we have further subtracted payroll costs and estimates of selected supplementary employee costs, maintenance and repair costs (other than salaries and wages to own employees), insurance premiums, rental payments, and property taxes.[3] The dollar figure remaining after these subtractions is, in effect, total gross profits plus quasi-rents (depreciation).[4] This total dollar margin figure was then divided by the value of shipments to give the percentage price-cost margin, which we take as an indicator of the difference between average price and average cost as a percentage of average price.

Values of the margin index computed as a weighted average of all four-digit industries within each two-digit industry group are shown in the last column of table 13. These figures were computed directly from the 1958 Census data, using all reported industries, because changes in classification among two-digit industries between 1954 and 1958 were not signifi-

---

[3] Estimates of these costs (other than payroll) have been made from the data in a sample survey, "Supplementary Inquiries for 1957," conducted as a part of the 1958 Census of Manufactures program. Data on these costs are not regularly subtracted by the Census in determining value added. We made use of estimates from the survey to obtain a better estimate of the margin between total receipts and total costs.

[4] This total margin figure does, however, include certain additional expenditures: advertising, developmental and research services provided by other establishments, and services of outside consultants. (For a detailed explanation, see U.S. Bureau of the Census, *U.S. Census of Manufactures: 1958. Vol. II, Industry Statistics, Part 1, Major Groups 20 to 28*, 1961, Appendix D, p. D–12.) Although the inclusion of some of the latter items in the total may be arguable, three points, at least, may be adduced to justify this procedure: many of the items (*e.g.*, services of outside consultants) are extremely small in relation to the totals involved; others (*e.g.*, advertising expenditures) are likely to be profit determined to an important degree; and a more refined measure of margins suitable for comparison with sales and concentration figures seems impossible to obtain on an interindustry basis from available data. Harberger has argued that for advertising expense it may be appropriate to include at least part as a sort of quasimonopoly profit. Arnold C. Harberger, "Monopoly and Resource Allocation," *American Economic Review*, Vol. XLIV, No. 2 (May, 1954), pp. 77–87. And Telser has found that concentration and advertising outlays as a percentage of sales are very weakly associated. L. G. Telser, "Advertising and Competition," *Journal of Political Economy*, Vol. LXXII, No. 6 (December, 1964), pp. 537–562.

cant. However, in the subsequent analysis of four-digit industry data it was necessary to exclude four-digit industries for which changes had occurred such that concentration measured on a 1954 definitional basis would not reflect the structure of the industry reported by the Census for 1958.

RELATIONSHIP BETWEEN PROFITABILITY AND CONCENTRATION

Results of a simple regression analysis of average profit and concentration data for two-digit major industry groups for 1958 are shown in the upper half of table 14, and results

TABLE 14   RESULTS OF REGRESSION ANALYSIS: AVERAGE CONCENTRATION RATIOS AND PROFIT RATES, TWO-DIGIT INDUSTRY GROUPS, 1958 AND 1956–1960

Profit measure (dependent variable)	Regression co-efficient for concentration variable	Constant term	r^2
1958 profits			
Before taxes:			
Percent of sales	.11 [a]	3.54	.34
Percent of assets	.12 [a]	6.26	.41
Percent of shareholders' equity	.19 [a]	9.47	.43
After taxes:			
Percent of sales	.05 [c]	2.03	.18
(excluding industry 29)	(.06) [a]	(1.60)	(.33)
Percent of assets	.06 [a]	3.21	.37
Percent of shareholders' equity	.10 [a]	4.78	.45
Average 1956–60 profits			
Before taxes:			
Percent of sales	.12 [a]	4.11	.34
Percent of assets	.12 [a]	7.67	.49
Percent of shareholders' equity	.20 [a]	11.85	.53
After taxes:			
Percent of sales	.05 [c]	2.44	.18
(excluding industry 29)	(.06) [b]	(1.99)	(.32)
Percent of assets	.06 [a]	4.17	.37
Percent of shareholders' equity	.09 [a]	6.40	.49

[a] Significant at 1 percent level.
[b] Significant at 5 percent level.
[c] Significant at 10 percent level.

for the 1956–1960 period in the lower half. For each period six profit measures were analyzed, and a significant positive association was found for each pair of variables. The statistical results are significant at the 1 percent level in ten of these regressions, and at the 10 percent level in the two instances in which after-tax profits as a percentage of sales were the dependent variables. This lower significance level is due to the large deviation of observed and expected values for the Petroleum and Coal Products group (SIC 29). The abnormal status of this group undoubtedly results from its unusual capital structure and special tax position, as well as from the inclusion of revenues from crude oil production and international operations in the data for the domestic refining industry. When an additional analysis of after-tax profits as a percentage of sales was made excluding this industry, the coefficient of determination increased substantially, and the significance level of the results improved from the 10 percent level to the 1 percent level for the 1958 data and to the 5 percent level for the average 1956–1960 profit rates.

The largest correlation coefficients were found between concentration and profits, both before and after taxes, as a percentage of equity. However, all the coefficients of determination support an inference of strong association. The pattern of association may be observed in figures 7 and 8. In the former, the weakest relationship—after-tax profits as a percentage of sales, 1956–1960—is shown in two regression lines, one including and one excluding the Petroleum and Coal Products industry. In figure 8, data for the strongest relationship—before-tax profits as a percentage of equity, 1956–1960—are plotted, along with the fitted regression line.

In summary, this set of computations indicates that an increase of 10 percentage points in the weighted average concentration index is associated with an increase of 1.1 percent in profits before taxes as a percentage of sales, and an increase of .5 percent in profits after taxes as a percentage of sales. The corresponding figures for profits as a percent-

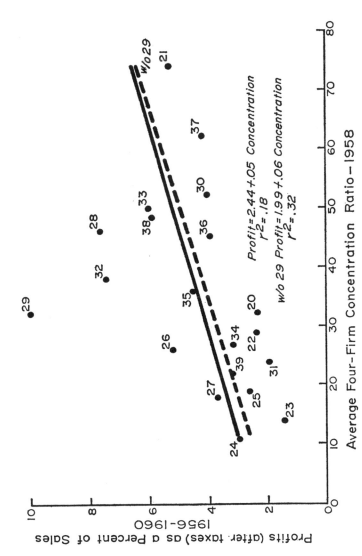

Fig. 7. Concentration and profits as percentage of sales, major SIC industry groups.

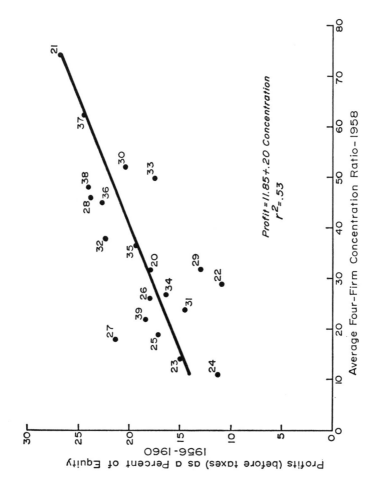

Fig. 8. Concentration and profits as percentage of equity, major SIC industry groups.

age of assets are 1.2 and .6 percent, and for stockholders' equity, 1.9 and 1.0 percent. When the unusual profits-sales relationship in petroleum in excluded, concentration as measured here explains from 32 percent to 53 percent of the variation in the several profit indicators among major industry groups.

Measured profitability might differ among industries primarily because of differences in their capital-output ratios. Even if rates of profit on capital were everywhere equalized, we would expect an association between capital-output ratios and profits as a percentage of sales. If high capital-output ratios are associated with high absolute capital requirements that might constitute barriers to entry, we might also expect a positive relationship between these ratios and the rate-of-return measures.

In order to examine these two hypotheses, the average capital-output ratio for each major industry group has been added to concentration as a second explanatory variable and the regression analysis has been repeated. Values for the capital-output ratios were obtained by dividing the total gross book value of assets in each industry, as of December 31, 1957, by the total value of shipments for 1958.[5] The regression results are given in table 15. The first hypothesis is readily confirmed by the statistical results. Profits as a percentage of sales, for both periods, and both before and after taxes, show a significant positive association with capital-output ratios. The results in table 15, compared with those in table 14, indicate that the addition of the capital-output ratio as an explanatory variable increases the coefficient of determination substantially in all four instances. The capital-output ratio also showed a significant statistical association with after-tax profits as a percentage of assets, al-

---

[5] Data on total gross book value of assets were obtained from U.S. Bureau of the Census, *U.S. Census of Manufactures: 1958. Vol. I* . . . , pp. 9–3 to 9–23. Value of shipments data were computed from U.S. Congress, Senate, Subcommittee on Antitrust and Monopoly, Committee on the Judiciary, *Concentration Ratios* . . . , Table 2.

TABLE 15   RESULTS OF REGRESSION ANALYSIS: AVERAGE
CONCENTRATION RATIOS, PROFIT RATES, AND CAPITAL-OUTPUT
RATIOS, TWO-DIGIT INDUSTRY GROUPS, 1958 AND 1956–1960

| Profit measure (dependent variable) | Regression coefficient for independent variable | | Constant term | R^2 |
	Concentration ratio	Capital-output ratio		
1958 profits				
Before taxes:				
Percent of sales	.08 [a]	.08 [a]	−1.44	.68
Percent of assets	.12 [a]	−.01	6.80	.42
Percent of shareholders' equity	.21 [a]	−.06	12.82	.50
After taxes:				
Percent of sales	.03 [c]	.08 [a]	−2.39	.78
Percent of assets	.05 [b]	.02 [c]	1.76	.47
Percent of shareholders' equity	.09 [a]	.01	4.04	.46
Average 1956–60 profits				
Before taxes:				
Percent of sales	.08 [a]	.10 [a]	−1.72	.75
Percent of assets	.12 [a]	.01	7.17	.49
Percent of shareholders' equity	.21 [a]	−.04	14.32	.57
After taxes:				
Percent of sales	.03 [c]	.08 [a]	−2.39	.83
Percent of assets	.05 [a]	.03 [b]	2.21	.57
Percent of shareholders' equity	.09 [a]	.02	5.25	.53

[a] Significant at 1 percent level.
[b] Significant at 5 percent level.
[c] Significant at 10 percent level.

though the increases in R^2 values were relatively smaller. No
significant association was found in the other six analyses of
assets and equity data. We therefore conclude that the possible independent impact of capital-intensity on the
profits-capital relationship suggested by the second hypothesis above is not strongly indicated by the data.

IMPACT OF LARGE INDUSTRIES

The foregoing results, together with those of previous studies, lead us to conclude that there is a fairly strong statistical association between average concentration levels and aggregate profit experience among major industry groups. This statistical result might reflect a much stronger underlying association between concentration and profits in the largest industries within each of the groups. The reasoning is as follows: The weighted average concentration indexes are constructed to give greater importance to the larger industries. The same industries may also be the primary determinants of industry group profits either because of their size in the total or because they occupy a leadership or pattern-setting role within their groups, to which the smaller industries, regardless of concentration, adapt.

To examine this problem we have identified the largest four-digit industries within each two-digit industry group and have analyzed the association between average concentration in these industries and average profit rates for the group as a whole. We identified "large" industries as those necessary to account for 15 percent, 25 percent, and 50 percent of the value of shipments of each of the twenty two-digit industry groups in 1958. In each instance we computed the weighted average concentration ratio for the large industries and regressed that index on the average two-digit group 1958 profit rates used above. The results are given in table 16; for comparative purposes, the last two columns reproduce the results shown in table 14. The arithmetic impact of the large industries would be reflected in equivalent statistical results in the two tables. A leadership role for the large industries would be indicated by stronger results in table 16 than in table 14; that is, profit rates for the entire group would be more closely associated with concentration in the large industries than with average concentration in the group as a whole.

The tabulated results give no indication of the potential

TABLE 16 RESULTS OF REGRESSION ANALYSIS: PROFIT RATES AND AVERAGE CONCENTRATION RATIOS FOR LARGEST INDUSTRIES

Profit measure (dependent variable)	Minimum number of industries required to account for:							
	15 percent of industry value of shipments		25 percent of industry value of shipments		50 percent of industry value of shipments		100 percent of industry value of shipments [1]	
	Regression coefficient for concentration	r^2	Regression coefficient for concentration	r^2	Regression coefficient for concentration	r^2	Regression coefficient for concentration	r^2
1958 profits								
Before taxes:								
Percent of sales	.05	.11	.06 [c]	.16	.07 [c]	.20	.11 [a]	.34
Percent of assets	.06 [c]	.19	.07 [b]	.22	.07 [b]	.25	.12 [a]	.41
Percent of share-holders' equity	.10 [b]	.25	.11 [b]	.27	.12 [b]	.29	.19 [a]	.43
After taxes:								
Percent of sales	.02	.05	.03	.08	.03	.10	.05 [c]	.18
Percent of assets	.03 [c]	.16	.03 [c]	.19	.04 [b]	.22	.06 [a]	.37
Percent of share-holders' equity	.05 [b]	.24	.06 [b]	.27	.06 [b]	.29	.10 [a]	.45

[1] From table 14. [a] Significant at 1 percent level. [b] Significant at 5 percent level. [c] Significant at 10 percent level.

leadership role of the large industries within their groups. On the contrary, the associations between average concentration in the large industries and group profit rates are uniformly weaker than associations between average group concentration and profit rates. One possible reason for this result is that large industries tend to be less concentrated than small industries. A second possibility is that the return-equalizing operations of the capital market may work much more efficiently on the large industries, keeping their rates of return in rough equivalence over time, whereas the smaller industries are more apt to display widely dispersed profit results, reflecting the impact of concentration, market size, capital requirements, and other factors. At any rate, the hypothesis that the large industries dominate the profit experience of their major groups is explicitly rejected on the basis of this analysis.

AVERAGE CONCENTRATION AND PRICE-COST MARGINS

The percentage gross profit margin on sales is measured as the difference between total revenues and variable costs expressed as a percentage of revenues. This indicator of profitability has the conceptual advantage of corresponding directly, under certain assumptions set forth in Chapter I, to the price-cost relationship dealt with in the theory of competition and monopoly. This index can be computed for the same four-digit industry classifications for which concentration data are available for 1958. We analyzed the association between the margin index computed for the two-digit major industry groups and the other measures of profitability used above for those groups, and then examined the association between the margin index and average concentration levels among the industry groups. The results of the latter analysis are to be compared both with the profits-concentration results presented earlier in this chapter, and with the results of our analysis of concentration and margins among four-digit industries in the next chapter.

Our data for price-cost margins in the twenty groups were

given in table 13, along with the data for the previously analyzed profitability measures. Simple correlation results between the margin series and each of the other profitability measures are shown in table 17. Using the data for all twenty two-digit groups, margins show the closest association with profits before taxes as a percentage of assets and equity. With the exception of profits after taxes as a percentage of sales, the values of the other coefficients of determination show significant but much weaker relationships. These results, however, are heavily influenced by the low margin and high rates of return computed for the Petroleum and

TABLE 17   CORRELATION OF 1958 PRICE-COST MARGINS WITH OTHER PROFIT MEASURES, TWO-DIGIT INDUSTRY GROUPS

Profit measure (dependent variable)	Coefficient of determination (r^2)—price-cost margin related to each profit measure	
	All 2-digit industry groups	Excluding petroleum and coal products group
1958 profits		
Before taxes:		
Percent of sales	.344 [a]	.625 [a]
Percent of assets	.702 [a]	.748 [a]
Percent of shareholders' equity	.687 [a]	.686 [a]
After taxes:		
Percent of sales	.063	.589 [a]
Percent of assets	.354 [a]	.745 [a]
Percent of shareholders' equity	.430 [a]	.715 [a]
1956–1960 profits		
Before taxes:		
Percent of sales	.280 [b]	.562 [a]
Percent of assets	.692 [a]	.733 [a]
Percent of shareholders' equity	.677 [a]	.655 [a]
After taxes:		
Percent of sales	.049	.533 [a]
Percent of assets	.325 [b]	.724 [a]
Percent of shareholders' equity	.423 [a]	.696 [a]

[a] Significant at 1 percent level.   [b] Significant at 5 percent level.

Coal Products group. If this group is removed from the data, the association between the margin index and the other measures of profitability—including, very importantly, after-tax profits as a percentage of sales—is quite high. It is also notable that the results for 1956–1960 are not greatly different from those for 1958 alone. Thus we conclude that

TABLE 18　Results of Regression Analysis: Price-cost Margins Related to Average Concentration and Capital-output Ratios, 1958

| Number of 2-digit industry groups | Regression coefficient for independent variable (t ratios in parentheses) | | Constant term | R^2 |
	Average concentration ratio	Capital-output ratio		
20	.16 [b] (2.14)	—	12.00	.20
	.17 [b] (2.10)	−.02 (−.28)	12.66	.21
19 (excluding SIC 29)	.16 [b] (2.29)	—	12.89	.24
	.15 [b] (2.20)	.02 (.28)	12.32	.24

[b] Significant at 5 percent level.

the margin index measures substantially the same industry characteristic as the other measures of profitability in industry groups other than Petroleum and Coal Products.

The data for average concentration levels and margins for the two-digit groups are plotted in figure 9, and regression results are shown in table 18. For all two-digit groups, the relationship between margins and concentration is significant at the 5 percent level. There is no significant association between margins and the capital-output ratio. When the Petroleum and Coal Products group is excluded from the analysis, the results are not significantly different.

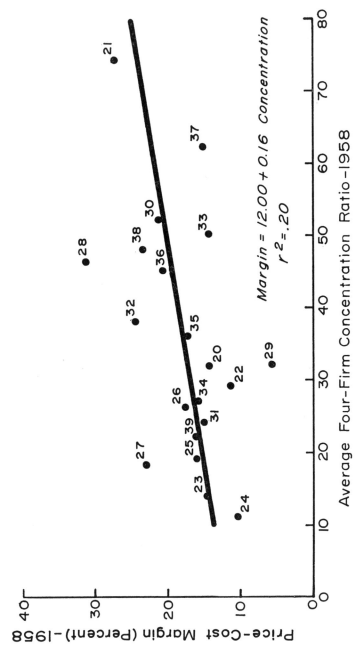

Fig. 9. Concentration and price-cost margins, major SIC industry groups.

The results for margins and concentration alone are weaker than those obtained above for concentration in relation to other profit measures, and the failure of the capital-output ratio to add substantially to the explanatory power of the regression contrasts sharply with our previous findings. There are several possible explanations of these discrepancies. One is that the margin index is a less reliable indicator of profitability than the other rates of return; if so, any relationship found between concentration and margins would tend to understate the relationship between concentration and rates of return. On the contrary, it might be argued that the margin index is a better indicator of the effect of monopoly on price,[6] and that the weaker results obtained from this analysis are a more accurate reflection of economic reality. In addition, it might be that these discrepancies exist only in aggregate data in which there is substantial double counting of intraindustry shipments and costs in the calculation of margins. Double counting does not occur in the profits, assets, and equity data to a comparable extent, nor does it occur in the margin computations for four-digit industries.

Whatever the explanation for the differences among the several profitability measures and among their relationships to average levels of concentration in the two-digit industry groups, the major conclusion from this analysis is that the profitability measures are moderately well correlated, and that the margin index is associated with average concentration levels in substantially the same way as are the other measures of profitability. Judging from these results, we conclude that an analysis of interindustry concentration and margin relationships should yield results indicative of associations between concentration and other measures of profitability. If the results of the margin analysis are biased, it is probably in the direction of weaker associations between

---

[6] Cf. Schwartzman, *op. cit.; and* Harberger, *op. cit.*

concentration and profitability than other profit measures would reveal.

CONTINUITY OF RELATIONSHIPS

The relationships between average concentration and profitability indicators for the major industry groups found in this analysis appear to be most accurately described as continuous functions over the range of the data. There is no evidence of the "distinct break" found in some analyses of more narrowly categorized data. This apparent continuity might be attributed to the high level of aggregation and the relatively narrow range of the data. Only one of the major industry groups (Tobacco) has an average concentration ratio above the 70 percent level. Division of the data into more and less concentrated subgroupings at almost any arbitrarily selected intermediate concentration level (e.g., 40 percent) will yield significant differences in mean profit rates or margins between the discrete categories. However, the figures in this chapter strongly suggest that the associations between the paired variables in each case should be conceived in terms of a continuous progression rather than a dichotomous distinction.

IV

Concentration and Price-Cost Margins in Census Industries

The preceding chapter reported an analysis of the relationship between concentration levels and price-cost margins among major manufacturing industry groups. Although an a priori important variable—the capital-output ratio—was introduced into the analysis, and statistically significant results were obtained, the substantive import of these findings is clouded by the high level of aggregation. The two-digit industry groups are composed of many diverse component industries, and the groups differ in degree of internal diversity as well as in size, age, pattern of technological and market history, and so on. The concentration indexes used in the preceding analysis had to be constructed by combining indexes specifically relating to the constituent industries; the validity of these combined indexes as indicators of differences in effective concentration levels among the major groups may be questioned. Thus it seemed desirable to extend the analysis on the basis of more sharply delineated industries, which may in turn be cross-classified for analytical purposes on the basis of their known or assumed common characteristics.

The ideal procedure would be to establish one's own standards of industry definition so that the terms "industry" and "market" would correspond, in Marshallian fashion, and then to cross-classify these "ideal" industries on the basis of full information about their potentially important characteristics. Such a procedure cannot, however, be attempted if a large sample is to be obtained, and perhaps cannot be adopted at all because of the intractability of the data and the inadequacy of our basic information and concepts. Therefore we are forced to rely on the SIC system and on Census data compiled on that basis, with only minor *ad hoc* adjustments.[1] Whatever the deficiencies of this category system, it is the basis for the largest available collection of data. Our analysis of this data constitutes a test of the value of the information being compiled by this system for this type of analysis.

The entire population of four-digit Census industries might be treated as a single collection of observations for analytical purposes, or this large collection might be broken down into subgroups on the basis of known or assumed common characteristics likely to affect the concentration-margin relationship. Among such characteristics, the least easy to observe accurately and express quantitatively are those associated with the unique history and development of each major segment of industry. The age, record of technological change, level and pattern of change of demand, and interindustry position of each group of economic units we identify as an "industry" are, in part, unique and not comparable among industries in even an ordinal fashion. However, these elusive but important features of industry structure, often difficult to describe in general terms, are apt to be more similar among industries closely related in terms of products, technology, or specific sources of demand than among industries selected at random from the entire industry population. For this reason we have attempted to control for some of these sources of interindustry diversity by grouping the available four-digit industries into their respective two-digit major industry groups for purposes of cross-sectional analysis. Of course, it is not to be expected that all the four-digit industries within any two-digit group will be alike with respect to all these qualitative,

---

[1] For detailed explanation, see U.S. Bureau of the Budget, *SIC Manual,* 1957; for a critique, see McKie, *op. cit.*

institutional, and historical features. However, the SIC procedure represents a reasonably acceptable choice among the available alternatives; and the four-digit industries within each major group are, with a few exceptions, more similar in important respects than many alternative collections of industry observations would be. We have therefore undertaken a detailed analysis of the concentration-margin relationship among four-digit industries within two-digit major industry groups. The results of this analysis are reported in this chapter, followed by additional results obtained from other groupings of the four-digit industry data.

DATA AND VARIABLES

The concentration statistics for 1958 were computed on the basis of the industry definitions used in the 1954 Census and concentration reports to permit comparability between the two sets of concentration indexes. There was, however, a significant revision of the SIC definitions in 1957, and thus the 1958 concentration data do not always correspond directly to the 1958 Census industries. To use the two sets of data in combination it was necessary to exclude industries for which definitional change had resulted in substantial noncomparability. All four-digit manufacturing industries were analyzed both in terms of definitional change and in terms of numerical differences in the same statistics (e.g., number of establishments, value of shipments) computed for 1958 on both the 1958 and the 1954 classification basis. Out of the total of 426 four-digit manufacturing industries reported in 1958, we found 288 industries for which both Census and concentration data were available on a comparable basis. These 288 industries were then classified according to their two-digit major industry groups, and all two-digit industry groups containing fifteen or more four-digit industries for which data were available were selected for detailed analysis. There were ten such major industry groups, totaling 213 four-digit industries. The industry groups and the distribution of four-digit industries among them are shown in table 19. Data for all 288 four-digit industries are listed in Appendix A.

Our analysis focuses on the relationship between the share of the four largest firms in the total shipments of a Census industry and the average price-cost margin in that industry. The computation of the price-cost margins has

TABLE 19   MAJOR INDUSTRY GROUPS AND NUMBER OF CONSTITUENT FOUR-DIGIT INDUSTRIES USED IN CROSS-SECTION ANALYSIS

Industry group	SIC code	Number of 4-digit industries
Food and kindred products	20	32
Textile mill products	22	17
Apparel and related products	23	24
Chemicals and allied products	28	19
Stone, clay and glass products	32	23
Primary metal industries	33	15
Fabricated metal products	34	20
Machinery, except electrical	35	22
Electrical machinery	36	18
Miscellaneous manufacturing	39	23
Total		213

been explained in Chapter III; in effect, we measure total gross profits plus quasi-rents (depreciation) before taxes and divide that figure by the value of shipments for the industry. This is an approximation for the desired statistic, the difference between price and average cost as a percentage of price.

The importance of the capital-output ratio as an explanation of differences in the concentration-profits relationship among industries has been discussed, and estimates of this ratio for each industry have been included in the analysis reported here. Using Census data, we have taken the ratio of gross book value of assets to value of shipments as the estimate of this variable.

Several additional variables suggested themselves as potential factors in the explanation of differences in interindustry profitability. However, only one of those examined proved to be of sufficient importance to merit detailed discussion here. Fuchs, Stigler, and others have called attention to the importance of differences in the geographic scope of markets in the interpretation of concentration data. Since the available concentration indexes are computed on a national basis, they may tend to understate the effective level of concentration in industries with sharply defined regional or local markets. Our statistical test of the concentration-margin relationship implies that concentration measures are equally valid for all industries; hence this difference in the geographical extent of markets had to be taken into account in our analysis. Unfortunately, there is no direct way to rank industries according to the relative importance of regional versus national markets. We can, however, measure the extent to which the productive facilities and output of industries are centralized in a few locations or scattered among many. If we assume that the demand for industry products is distributed roughly in proportion to the distribution of population among fairly large regions, then the difference between the percentage distribution of population (demand) and output (supply) within each region is an indicator of the existence of interregional, or roughly "national," rather than localized markets. Conversely, if industry output in each region is approximately proportional to regional demand as indicated by population, it is possible that separable regional or local markets are in operation. Admittedly, this is a crude indicator which may be applied only for fairly large geographic areas and broadly defined industries. It neglects the impact of transportation costs and the strength of interarea competitive pressures other than transshipment. However, it can be computed from readily available data, and it has the advantage of recognizing gradients between the extremes of national and local industries, rather than imposing dichotomous categories on continuous phenomena.

In order to calculate the specific statistic used in our analysis, the percentage of total value of shipments for each industry accounted for by establishments within each of the four broad Census regions—Northeast, North Central, South, and West—was computed, and the percentage distribution of 1958 population among the same regions was determined. The index of geographic dispersion for each industry is calculated as the sum of the absolute differences between these two percentages. The lower this index, the greater the degree of geographic dispersion of the industry, and hence the greater the likelihood of local and regional markets. We therefore hypothesize that the lower this index, the higher the expected price-cost margins for any given level of national concentration.[2]

ANALYTICAL PROCEDURE

The relationship between price-cost margins and the three characteristics of industry structure described above was analyzed within a regression framework; linear functions were fitted by the method of least squares. It is assumed that the data may be treated as a sample from a population of years and that statistical estimation and testing procedures are appropriate.

A separate cross-sectional analysis was made for the component four-digit industries within each two-digit major industry group. In each analysis, two linear regression equations were fitted, as follows:

$$(1) \quad Y_1 = a + bX_1$$
$$(2) \quad Y_1 = a + bX_1 + cX_2 + dX_3$$

where

---

[2] The importance of the geographic spread of an industry in this context also has been explored by Fuchs. As a measure of geographic dispersion, he employed a "coefficient of scatter," defined as the smallest number of states required to account for 75 percent of industry value added. See Fuchs, *op. cit.*, pp. 287–288.

Y_1 = price-cost margin
X_1 = concentration ratio
X_2 = index of geographic dispersion
X_3 = capital-output ratio

Regression coefficients and coefficients of determination are reported for each industry, and the net regression relationship between concentration and price-cost margins is illustrated graphically.

The illustrated net regressions between margins and concentration are computed from the estimated multiple regression equations by holding the variables X_2 and X_3 constant at their mean values and predicting a value for Y_1 on the basis of variations in X_1 alone. The linear relationships illustrated in the figures are thus two-dimensional projections of a four-variable function. The figures also show the differences (residuals) between the actual concentration-margin observations and the values predicted from the four-variable function, plotted as deviations from the net regression line.

This procedure is illustrated in figure 10 with the following hypothetical case:

The fitted four-variable function is:

$$Y_1 = 10 + .4X_1 - .2X_2 + .2X_3$$

Mean values are:

$$\overline{X}_2 = 5$$
$$\overline{X}_3 = 15$$

Substituting the mean values yields:

$$Y_1 = 10 + .4X_1 - 1 + 3$$
$$Y_1 = 12 + .4X_1$$

This last function is the net regression plotted in figure 10.

Now suppose that the sets of actual observations used to estimate the function included the following:

	Y_1	X_1	X_2	X_3
Industry A	20	25	6	14
Industry B	40	66	4	16

From these data, values of Y_1 for each industry can be predicted from the four-variable function, and the difference (residual) between the actual and predicted values can be obtained. These residuals, positive for Industry A and nega-

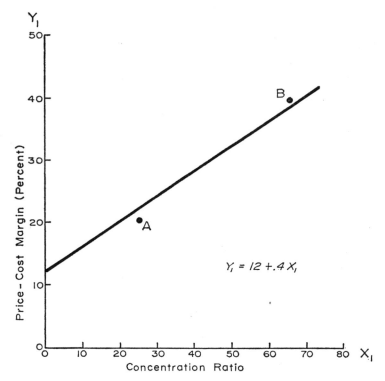

Fig. 10. Hypothetical illustration of net regression relationship.

tive for Industry B, are then plotted as deviations from the net regression line in figure 10; they are shown as points A and B. The data required for this construction are as follows:

	Actual (1)	Predicted (2)	Residual (3) = (1) − (2)	Net regression (4)	Plotted point (5) = (4) + (3)
Industry A	20	21.6	−1.6	22	20.4
Industry B	40	38.8	+1.2	38.4	39.6

The net regression line is plotted to illustrate the relationship between concentration and margins with values of other variables held constant. The plot of residuals around the net regression line is a projection in two dimensions of the scatter of the actual data about the four-dimensional regression surface. It is thus a reflection of the goodness-of-fit of the four-variable function and an illustration of the specific sources of major deviations.

STATISTICAL RESULTS

The statistical analysis of cross-section data within each of the ten industry groups yielded diverse results. A statistically significant and positive association between margins and concentration was observed in six groups:

SIC code	Industry
20	Food and Kindred Products
32	Stone, Clay and Glass Products
33	Primary Metal Industries
34	Fabricated Metal Products
36	Electrical Machinery
39	Miscellaneous Manufacturing

The remaining four major industry groups did not yield evidence of such a relationship:

SIC code	Industry
22	Textile Mill Products
23	Apparel and Related Products
28	Chemicals and Allied Products
35	Machinery, except Electrical

TABLE 20 RESULTS OF REGRESSION ANALYSIS, SIX INDUSTRY GROUPS

Industry group	Number of 4-digit industries	Equation	Concentration ratio (X_1)	Geographic dispersion (X_2)	Capital-output ratio (X_3)	Constant term	R^2
				Regression coefficients of independent variables (t ratios in parentheses)			
Food and kindred products (SIC 20)	32	1	.31 [a] (4.49)	—	—	6.05	.40
		2	.41 [a] (7.09)	−.13 [a] (4.03)	.19 [b] (2.48)	5.06	.69
Stone, clay and glass products (SIC 32)	23	1	.16 [b] (2.61)	—	—	15.93	.25
		2	.15 [b] (2.47)	−.09 (1.49)	.07 (1.38)	15.99	.42
Primary metal industries (SIC 33)	15	1	.20 [b] (2.60)	—	—	4.74	.34
		2	.14 (1.30)	−.03 (.30)	.08 (.77)	4.66	.38

TABLE 20 (CONTINUED)

Industry group	Number of 4-digit industries	Equation	Regression coefficients of independent variables (t ratios in parentheses)			Constant term	R^2
			Concentration ratio (X_1)	Geographic dispersion (X_2)	Capital-output ratio (X_3)		
Fabricated metal products (SIC 34)	20	1	.13 [b] (2.18)	—	—	14.73	.21
		2	.05 (1.53)	.20 [a] (7.12)	−.20 [b] (2.54)	13.59	.81
Electrical machinery (SIC 36)	18	1	.11 (1.46)	—	—	16.36	.12
		2	.15 [b] (2.17)	−.14 [c] (1.85)	−.18 [c] (1.83)	28.99	.40
Miscellaneous manufacturing (SIC 39)	23	1	.11 [b] (2.41)	—	—	16.42	.22
		2	.09 [b] (2.42)	−.05 [a] (2.95)	.004 (.18)	20.83	.46

[a]Significant at 1 percent level.   [b] Significant at 5 percent level.   [c] Significant at 10 percent level.

The statistical findings for the first six industry groups are shown in table 20 and illustrated in figures 11–16. Results for the remaining four groups are shown in table 21. All the basic data are tabulated in Appendix A. We now consider the results for each industry group in turn.

Food and Kindred Products

The Food and Kindred Products industry group contains the largest sample of four-digit Census industries of any major group classification. Two *ad hoc* adjustments reduced to thirty-two the number of component industries for which data were available. One industry, manufactured ice (SIC 2097), was excluded, and two industries, cane sugar refining (SIC 2062) and beet sugar (SIC 2063), were combined by a weighted averaging of the concentration indexes and summing of the other relevant data.

The analysis of data for this group of industries strongly supports the hypothesis of a positive relationship between price-cost margins and concentration.[3] The regression coefficients of the concentration variable in both equations are positive and statistically significant at the 1 percent level. Concentration alone accounts for 40 percent of the variation in measured price-cost margins; and concentration, geographic dispersion, and capital-output ratios together account for almost 70 percent.

The net regression relationship ($Y_1 = 2.04 + .41X_1$) between concentration and margins is shown in figure 11, together with the differences (residuals) between actual and predicted values plotted as deviations from the line. In another study [4] we used a curvilinear function to describe the

---

[3] These findings were further confirmed by a more recent study: National Commission on Food Marketing, *The Structure of Food Manufacturing*, Technical Study No. 8, prepared by the staff of the Federal Trade Commission (Washington: U.S. Government Printing Office, 1966), Chap. VI.
[4] Collins and Preston, "Concentration and Price-Cost Margins in Food Manufacturing Industries," *Journal of Industrial Economics*, Vol. XIV, No. 3 (July, 1966), pp. 226–240.

same relationship; that function fitted to the present data yields the following results (t ratios in parentheses):

$$Y_1 = 15.699 - .274X_1 + .007X_1^2 - .121X_2 + .240X_3$$
$$\qquad\quad (1.45) \quad (3.75) \quad (4.62) \quad (3.68)$$
$$R^2 = .80$$

The curvilinear function thus yields a somewhat better explanation of the data than the linear function ($R^2 = .80$ as compared to $R^2 = .69$). However, curvilinear patterns were not indicated in all the cross-sectional data under analysis here, and we have restricted ourselves to linear functions to permit direct comparability among the results.

In three of the thirty-two food industries, the actual price-cost margin differs by more than 10 percentage points from the value predicted from the regression equation. These industries are identified by number in figure 11 and the differences (actual minus predicted values) are as follows:

2091	Cottonseed oil mills	−13.68
2062–63	Cane-beet sugar refining	−11.16
2043	Cereal preparations	+10.19

Although *ad hoc* arguments might be introduced for excluding any one of these industries from the analysis, the strength of the relationship even when they are included commands attention.

Both the index of geographic dispersion and the capital-output ratio show significant regression relationships in the food industries. The greater the geographic dispersion of the industry, the lower the index and the greater the likelihood of regional or local, rather than national, markets. Our a priori expectation is that the more dispersed the industry, and thus the lower the index, the higher will be the price-cost margin for any given level of national concentration. Thus a negative coefficient is expected and, for the food industries, a significant value is obtained. The capital-output ratio carries the expected positive sign—the greater the cap-

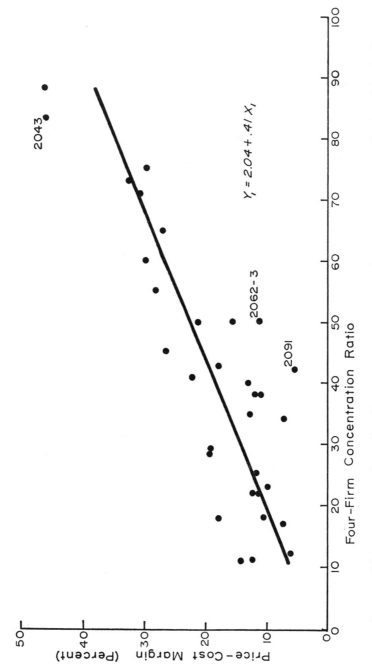

Fig. 11. Net regression relationship between concentration and price-cost margins—food and kindred products industries, 1958.

ital intensity, the greater the price-cost margin for any concentration level—and the coefficient is significant at the 5 percent level.

Stone, Clay and Glass Products

Statistical results for the Stone, Clay and Glass Products industries are considerably weaker than those for the food group. Concentration alone explains only 25 percent of the variation in price-cost margins among the twenty-three component industries, and neither geographic dispersion nor capital-output ratio shows a significant regression coefficient, although their addition to the analysis yields a significant increase in R^2. Evidently, both geographic dispersion and capital-output ratios fall just below our minimum levels of statistical significance. If the analysis is rerun with either of these variables excluded, the other variable reveals a regression coefficient significant at the 10 percent level, but the sign of the coefficient for X_3 is not as expected. The results of these computations are as follows (t ratios in parentheses):

$$Y_1 = 19.74 + .17X_1 - .12X_2$$
$$(3.01) \quad (1.95)$$
$$R^2 = .37$$

$$Y_1 = 12.07 + .13X_1 - .09X_3$$
$$(2.14) \quad (1.86)$$
$$R^2 = .36$$

The net regression for these industries is shown in figure 12, and the two industries with residuals greater than 10 percentage points are indicated:

| 3241 | Cement, hydraulic | +11.70 |
| 3263 | Earthenware food utensils | −14.29 |

Primary Metal Industries

The results for the Primary Metal Industries are very similar to those for the Stone, Clay and Glass Products

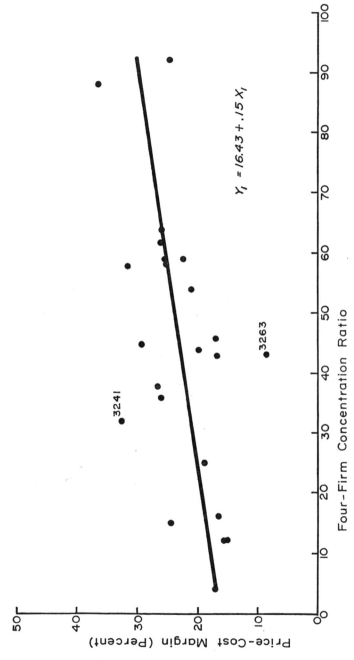

$Y_i = 16.43 + .15 X_i$

3241

3263

Four-Firm Concentration Ratio

Price-Cost Margin (Percent)

Fig. 12. Net regression relationship between concentration and price-cost margins—stone, clay and glass products industries, 1958.

group, except that the addition of geographic dispersion and capital-output ratios to the analysis reduces the significance of the regression coefficient for concentration itself. Concentration alone explains 34 percent of the variation in price-cost margins among the fifteen constituent industries, and the regression coefficient is significant at the 5 percent level. The addition of the other two variables slightly increases the value of R^2, but yields no regression coefficient significant at the 10 percent level or better.

Two of the fifteen industries show differences of more than 10 percentage points between their actual and predicted price-cost margin values (fig. 13):

3333	Primary zinc	−12.11
3339	Primary nonferrous metals, nec	+12.88

The inadequacy of the concentration ratio as an indicator of market structure for the many highly specialized products included in the latter industry is clearly indicated.

Fabricated Metal Products

In the Fabricated Metal Products group, concentration alone explains 21 percent of the variation in price-cost margins among the twenty component industries, and the regression coefficient is significant at the 5 percent level. However, when geographic dispersion and capital-output ratio are added to the analysis, concentration is no longer shown to be a significant variable, although the level of explanation for the entire function increases to 81 percent. The signs of the coefficients for the two additional variables are significant but are the reverse of those expected. Signs of significant coefficients are also reversed for geographic dispersion in the Apparel and Related Products industries group, and capital-output ratio in Electrical Machinery. In no other case are both signs reversed.

These paradoxical results are due primarily to the presence of extreme values for two industries. Although in eighteen of the twenty industries price-cost margins range from

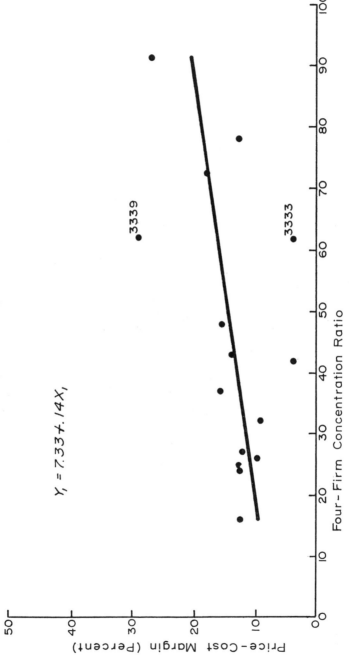

Fig. 13. Net regression relationship between concentration and price-cost margins—primary metal industries, 1958.

11 to 23 percent (a relatively narrow range, as the data in Appendix A indicate), in two very small industries (SIC 3421, cutlery, and SIC 3492, safes and vaults) the price-cost margins are above 35 percent. These industries show four-firm concentration levels of 53 and 91, respectively. Their presence in the data is sufficient to yield a significant association between margins and concentration when these two variables are considered alone. The index of geographic dispersion also shows extreme high values for these same industries, accounting for the positive relationship with concentration.

The net regression is shown in figure 14, although the slight positive slope illustrated is not significantly different from the horizontal.

Electrical Machinery

Results for the Electrical Machinery group contrast sharply with those in the two preceding groups. In this group of eighteen industries, concentration alone does not prove to be a significant explanatory variable for the variation in price-cost margins. However, when the other two variables are added to the analysis, each of them shows a regression coefficient significant at the 10 percent level, concentration itself proves to be significant at the 5 percent level, and an R^2 value of .40 is obtained. As table 20 indicates, this value for R^2 is comparable with that obtained in most of the other cases in which significant relationships were revealed. The sign of the coefficient of the capital-output ratio, however, is negative, as it is for Fabricated Metal Products.

The net regression is shown in figure 15, with the residuals plotted as deviations about the line. Only two of these are as great as 10 percentage points, and both are negative:

> 3636 Sewing machines −10.74
> 3691 Storage batteries −12.85

The former industry stands out as an anomaly in the basic data. It is one of the twelve industries with a concentration

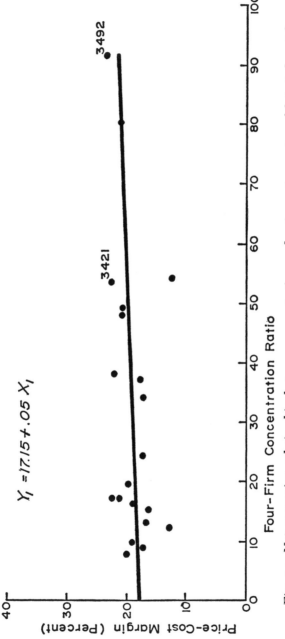

Fig. 14. Net regression relationship between concentration and price-cost margins—fabricated metal products industries, 1958.

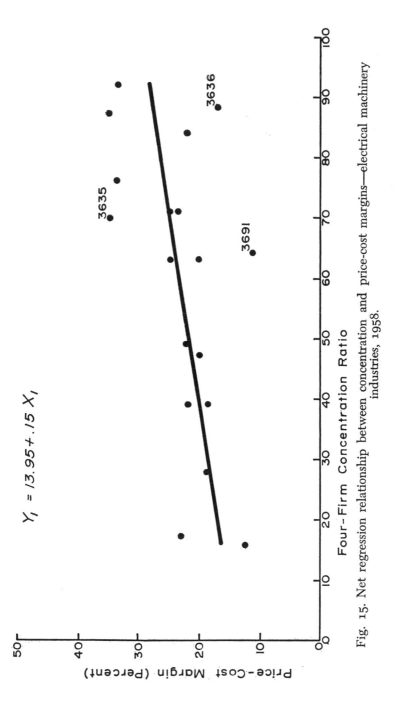

Fig. 15. Net regression relationship between concentration and price-cost margins—electrical machinery industries, 1958.

ratio over 80, and the average price-cost margin is only 5.71 percent. It represents a rare instance of a pairing of extreme values that is directly the reverse of a priori expectations in the entire collection of data for the 213 industries. The effect of international competition as an offset to domestic concentration may be surmised. The largest positive residual is that for SIC 3635, household vacuum cleaners, +9.76.

Miscellaneous Manufacturing

The twenty-three four-digit industries in this category include such products as jewelry, matches, office supplies, toys, and umbrellas. These industries clearly lack the broad similarity of raw materials, production technology, or inter-industry trading position characterizing most of the industries within other major industry groups. However, these industries present a worthwhile case for analysis because they have in common relatively small size and sharp industry definition, and they might be expected a priori to be characterized by more highly inelastic industry demands with respect to price.

The results for this heterogeneous group of industries indicate a positive association between concentration and margins. The regression coefficient for concentration is significant at the 5 percent level in both equations, and the two R^2 values are comparable to those in the preceding cases. The coefficient for geographic dispersion, although significant at the 1 percent level, is small, and no significant result for capital-output ratio is obtained. The surprisingly close fit of the function is indicated by the plot of the deviations around the net regression line in figure 16. The largest difference between actual and predicted price-cost margins is only 7 percentage points (SIC 3943, children's vehicles).

Four Additional Industries

Statistical results for the four additional industries for which cross-sectional analyses were made are shown in table 21. No significant association was found between concentra-

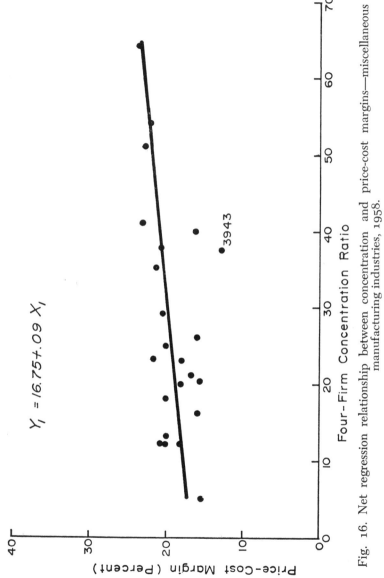

$Y_1 = 16.75 + .09 X_1$

Fig. 16. Net regression relationship between concentration and price-cost margins—miscellaneous manufacturing industries, 1958.

TABLE 21 RESULTS OF REGRESSION ANALYSIS, FOUR INDUSTRY GROUPS

| Industry group | Number of 4-digit industries | Equation | Regression coefficients of independent variables (t ratios in parentheses) | | | Constant term | R^2 |
			Concentration ratio (X_1)	Geographic dispersion (X_2)	Capital-output ratio (X_3)		
Textile mill products (SIC 22)	17	1	.05 (0.78)	—	—	11.47	.04
		2	.06 (1.30)	−.09 [a] (4.20)	−.11 (1.74)	22.76	.66
Apparel and related products (SIC 23)	24	1	−.02 (0.28)	—	—	15.50	.004
		2	.06 (0.70)	.05 [b] (2.35)	.03 (0.21)	9.15	.23
Chemicals and allied products (SIC 28)	19	1	−.09 (0.69)	—	—	32.13	.03
		2	−.06 (0.41)	.12 (1.31)	−.02 (0.21)	25.10	.13
Machinery, except electrical (SIC 35)	22	1	.07 (0.99)	—	—	15.54	.05
		2	.04 (0.43)	.06 (0.71)	−.06 (0.61)	15.04	.08

[a] Significant at 1 percent level.   [b] Significant at 5 percent level.

tion and margins, nor was any association found between margins and the capital-output ratio. In two instances, Textile Mill Products and Apparel and Related Products, small but significant coefficients were obtained for the index of geographic dispersion, but one of these (Apparel and Related Products) is not of the expected sign. Results for the Chemicals group are very strongly affected by the presence of two very high-margin and relatively low-concentration consumer goods industries (pharmaceuticals and toiletries) in a sample composed primarily of producer goods industries.

SUMMARY OF RESULTS, TEN INDUSTRY GROUPS

Our cross-sectional analysis of individual industry data for each of the ten major industry groups yielded highly diverse results. Some association between margins and concentration was found in six of the ten groups; no association was observed in four. Among the first six groups were three instances in which concentration and margins showed a significant regression relationship whether or not additional variables were included; in two instances only when concentration alone was included; and one instance only when the other two explanatory variables were included. Geographic dispersion, as measured by our index, proved to be a significant explanatory variable in six of the ten groups, although in two of these the sign was opposite to our expectations. The capital-output ratio proved to be a significant explanatory variable in only three cases, and in two of these the sign was the reverse of that expected. Although these results are too varied to permit a single sweeping conclusion to be drawn, the clear statistical significance and nonnegligible magnitudes of the associations between concentration and margins cannot be lightly dismissed. The six industry groups in which the relationship between concentration and margins is positive and significantly different from zero at the 5 percent level or better contain 131 of the 213 industries under analysis.

The disparities among our results for the several industries remain, however, perplexing. We would like to separate those disparities attributable to important differences in the operation of competitive forces, including foreign competition, from those due to interindustry differences of some other sort (e.g., differences in demand elasticities) or to inadequacies in the data. Our failure to observe a significant regression relationship in any particular collection of observations might be due to the lack of adequate dimension in the data. That is, we would not expect to find strong linear relationship in a closely bunched group of industry observations. The scatter of concentration values for the first six industries can be observed in figures 11–16; the data for all industries are given in Appendix A. For convenience in comparison, table 22 presents summary frequency distributions of concentration and margin levels in the ten groups and for the seventy-five additional industries. This table indicates that the Food and Kindred Products group, in which the strongest statistical associations were observed, includes not only the greatest number of individual industry observations but also a wide range of concentration and margin values. The Stone, Clay and Glass Products group, although smaller in number, displays a fairly wide scatter of values for both variables. At the opposite extreme is the Textile Mill Products group, which contains only seventeen industries, thirteen of which have concentration ratios of 40 or less, and sixteen of which have price-cost margins under 60 percent. Of course, some groups offering a fairly wide scatter of points do not reveal significant linear relationships for the variables under analysis; the Chemicals and Allied Products group is the best example of this.

ADDITIONAL RESULTS, FOUR-DIGIT INDUSTRIES

The statistical analysis has been repeated for the entire collection of 213 four-digit industries in the ten industry groups and for all 288 four-digit industries for which requi-

TABLE 22 Frequency Distributions and Ranges, Concentration Ratios and Margins, Four-digit Industries

	Food and kindred products	Stone, clay and glass products	Primary metals	Fabricated metals	Electrical machinery	Miscellaneous manufacturing	Textile mill products	Apparel and related products	Chemicals and allied products	Machinery, except electrical	Totals	Additional industries	Grand total
Number of 4-digit industries	32	23	15	20	18	23	17	24	19	22	213	75	288
Concentration Ratios													
0– 20	6	5	1	10	2	9	3	19	1	4	60	22	82
21– 40	11	4	6	4	3	10	10	4	5	6	63	24	87
41– 60	9	10	3	4	2	3	3	1	5	8	48	18	66
61– 80	4	2	4	1	7	1	1	0	7	3	30	8	38
81–100	2	2	1	1	4	0	0	0	1	1	12	3	15
High	88	92	91	91	92	64	68	41	93	87	93	97	97
Median	39	44	42	21	63	23	25	14	55	43	36	32	34
Low	11	4	16	5	16	5	7	3	18	7	3	6	3
Price-cost margin (percent)													
0– 9.99	7	1	4	0	1	0	3	1	0	2	19	7	26
10.0–19.99	13	8	8	15	6	15	13	21	6	11	116	47	163
20.0–29.99	7	12	2	3	8	8	1	2	6	7	56	17	73
30.0–39.99	4	1	1	2	3	0	0	0	4	2	17	3	20
40.0–49.99	1	1	0	0	0	0	0	0	1	0	3	1	4
50.0–	0	0	0	0	0	0	0	0	2	0	2	0	2
High	41.67	40.47	30.55	36.50	37.99	25.60	20.36	23.63	51.27	32.46	51.27	40.85	51.27
Median	18.41	22.26	12.39	17.30	22.80	19.68	12.81	14.49	25.88	18.34	17.53	16.47	17.22
Low	4.31	8.17	6.52	11.11	5.70	13.84	6.11	8.00	11.85	4.07	4.07	2.97	2.97

site data are available. The additional seventy-five industries are distributed among ten other major industry groups, no one of which contains a sufficient number of observations for detailed analysis (see Appendix A). The 288-industry sample was then cross-classified by broad capital-output and geographical dispersion categories, and regression results were computed for each of these subsamples. The latter computations were made to allow for the possibility that our estimates of both of these variables might be unnecessarily precise. That is, it may be relevant to separate highly capital-intensive industries, or geographically concentrated industries, or their opposites, from all others, but not to take account of fine (and possibly ill-measured) distinctions within these broad categories.

The data indicated that major clusters of values could be identified as follows:

> Index of geographic dispersion: Low (under 30), Medium (30–89.99), and High (90 and over).
> Capital-output ratio: Low (under 50 percent) and High (50 percent and over).

More than 60 percent of all the industries are in the "medium" geographic dispersion class, and 78 percent are in the "low" capital-output class. Almost exactly half (141) of the industries fall into both classes, and this group of industries has also been segregated for analysis.

The results of the computations are shown in table 23. The regression coefficients between concentration and price-cost margins are significant at the 5 percent level or better in all but one of the fifteen statistical analyses. The coefficients of determination range from .06 to .40; the latter involves an association between capital-output ratios and margins for the forty industries with very low indexes of geographic dispersion (i.e., highly regionalized industries). The only other instance of a variable other than concentration showing a significant relationship with margins in this treatment of the data is the negative association between

TABLE 23 RESULTS OF REGRESSION ANALYSIS, ALL FOUR-DIGIT INDUSTRIES

Group of industries	Number of 4-digit industries	Equation	Regression coefficients of independent variables			Constant term	R^2
			Concentration ratio (X_1)	Geographic dispersion (X_2)	Capital-output ratio (X_3)		
Industries in cross-sectional analysis	213	1	.153[a]	—	—	13.228	.18
		2	.143[a]	−.021	.019	14.323	.19
All available 4-digit industries	288	1	.125[a]	—	—	13.901	.12
		2	.122[a]	−.015	.011	14.598	.13
All industries classified by index of geographic dispersion							
Less than 30	40	1	.100[c]	—	—	15.923	.09
		1a	.031	—	.178[a]	10.586	.40
30–89.99	180	1	.123[a]	—	—	14.125	.11
		1a	.131[a]	—	−.026	14.764	.11
90 and over	68	1	.144[a]	—	—	12.222	.19
		1a	.173[a]	—	−.070	13.121	.21
All industries classified by capital-output ratio							
Under 50	225	1	.129[a]	—	—	13.597	.13
		1b	.129[a]	.002	—	13.451	.13
50 and above	63	1	.100[b]	—	—	15.814	.06
		1b	.106[b]	−.081[b]	—	20.241	.13
All industries with geographic dispersion 30–89.99 and capital-output ratio under 50	141	1	.137[a]	—	—	13.751	.12

Equation 1: $Y_1 = a + bX_1$,   Equation 1a: $Y_1 = a + bX_1 + cX_2 + dX_3$.
Equation 2: $Y_1 = a + bX_1 + cX_2 + dX_3$,   Equation 1b: $Y_1 = a + bX_1 + cX_2$.
[a] Significant at 1 percent level.   [b] Significant at 5 percent level.   [c] Significant at 10 percent level.

margins and the geographic dispersion index in the sixty-three industries with capital-output ratios above 50 percent. This result is consistent with our a priori expectations.

The statistical results for concentration and margins are only slightly stronger for the 213 industries used in the industry group subsamples than for the entire group of 288 industries. The value of .153 obtained for the regression coefficient in the first equation is very close to the median of significant coefficients obtained from the subsamples, and the values obtained for the 288 industry data collection are consistent with the tenor of our previous findings.

As expected, the grouping of industries into broad classes with respect to the other two explanatory variables has a substantial impact on the statistical results. Relatively weak associations between concentration and margins were found for industries with low indexes of geographic dispersion (regional industries). By contrast, relatively strong associations were found for industries with high geographic dispersion indexes. These are industries in which production is concentrated in a few locations compared with the broad regional distribution of the population, and which are therefore presumed to serve interregional, or roughly "national," markets from relatively concentrated sources of supply. It is precisely for these industries that we would expect the measured concentration data to be most relevant to economic concepts of industry structure, and thus it is significant that the results for these industries (which constitute less than 25 percent of the total) are comparable to the median cross-sectional results. When the industries are cross-classified by capital-output ratios, the more capital-intensive industries show a somewhat weaker relationship between concentration and margins than the less capital-intensive industries.

The results for industries with indexes of geographic dispersion in the medium range, for industries with capital-output ratios under 50 percent, and for industries with both characteristics are very close to the results for the 288-industry collection as a whole. This similarity would be anticipated because these industries constitute a large part of the total sample. However, it is reassuring to find that the relationships observed in the total collection are not due to the extreme values but are, in fact, found in a large subsample of data containing what might be called the normal range of values of the geographic and capital variables. These additional results thus tend to confirm our previous findings, as well as to indicate some industry characteristics that appear to weaken the concentration-margin relationship.

IMPACT OF DEMAND ELASTICITY

In Chapter I we noted that price-cost margins would vary among completely monopolized industries inversely with the price elasticity of industry demand. Does this relationship provide any explanation of the margin differences found in our data? Could the observed differences in margins be explained primarily in terms of differences in demand elasticities among industries all subject to the same degree of quasi-monopolistic behavior? Numerical estimates of industry demand elasticities on an appropriate classification basis are unattainable. However, the effect cited would depend upon substantial *differences* in elasticity values among industries, not on specific levels, and an inspection of the data provides some clues. In table 24 the twenty-six four-digit industries with price-cost margins above 30 percent are listed with their margins and concentration ratios. The margins computed for some of these industries are undoubtedly substantially affected by the inclusion of advertising expenditures. However, even a generous adjustment would leave all these industries in the high-margin category. In only four of the listed industries are four-firm concentration ratios below 50 percent.

Some of the textbook examples of inelastic demand industries may be noted in the table: chewing gum, distilled liquors, cigarettes, pharmaceuticals, toiletries, electric lamps. Highly inelastic demand should probably be expected also for such industrial products as carbon black and industrial gases, and for manufactured items such as safes, elevators, and typewriters. However, after these and other possible examples are noted, roughly half of the high-margin industries remain in which there is no a priori reason to

TABLE 24 INDUSTRIES WITH PRICE-COST MARGINS ABOVE 30 PERCENT

SIC industry		Margin	Concentration ratio
2043	Cereal preparations	38	83
2052	Biscuits and crackers	31	65
2073	Chewing gum	42	88
2085	Distilled liquors	34	60
2087	Flavorings	40	55
2111	Cigarettes	41	79
2131	Chewing and smoking tobacco	33	57
2646	Pressed and molded pulp goods	31	69
2731	Books	38	16
2813	Industrial gases	37	79
2816	Inorganic pigments	34	69
2818	Inorganic chemicals n.e.c.	32	55
2823-24	Cellulosic and organic fibers	32	78
2834	Pharmaceutical preparations	51	27
2844	Toilet preparations	51	29
2895	Carbon black	40	73
3241	Cement, hydraulic	40	32
3275	Gypsum products	40	88
3339	Primary nonferrous metals, n.e.c.	31	62
3421	Cutlery	37	53
3492	Safes and vaults	35	91
3534	Elevators and moving stairways	32	62
3572	Typewriters	31	79
3635, 3584	Vacuum cleaners	34	70
3641	Electric lamps	38	92
3652	Phonograph records	36	76

expect extreme demand inelasticity. Thus it would appear that the association between high concentration and high margins remains whether or not a priori differences in demand elasticities are taken into account. Properly measured, such differences—and other demand characteristics such as rate of market growth and income elasticity—may not be without effect on the concentration-margin relationship. However, our data do not provide any indication of the presence or magnitude of such effects.

CONTINUOUS FUNCTION OR DISTINCT BREAK?

Any sample of industries in which statistically significant regression results were obtained would be expected also to show a significant difference between average margins in appropriately defined subsamples of highly concentrated and less concentrated industries. It might therefore be argued that our regression results, although cast in terms of a continuous function, might as easily support the hypothesis of a discrete difference in price-cost relations between tight oligopoly and all other forms of industry structure. Indeed, when the observations are unevenly distributed over the range of values and the statistical results are relatively weak, dichotomous tests would seem to offer the firmer conclusion. This would be particularly persuasive if dichotomous tests yielded significant results for samples of data in which no continuous function was found.

In table 25 our four-digit industry data are examined for evidence of a distinct break in the concentration-margin relationship at the 50 percent and 70 percent concentration levels. The selection of any single level of concentration as sufficient to identify tight-oligopoly industries is, of course, arbitrary. However, significant differences were found for industries below and above the 70 percent level in the Schwartzman data, and this was the level of eight-firm concentration used as a breaking point in Bain's original study. The 50 percent level for four-firm concentration may correspond more directly to the 70 percent level for eight-firm concentration, and it also provides a further basis for comparison.

One industry group for which significant regression results were obtained (Miscellaneous Manufacturing) does

TABLE 25 AVERAGE PRICE-COST MARGINS FOR FOUR-DIGIT INDUSTRIES ABOVE AND BELOW 50 AND 70 PERCENT CONCENTRATION LEVELS

| | 4-firm concentration ratio ≦ 50 percent | | | | | 4-firm concentration ratio ≦ 70 percent | | | | |
| | Less than | | Equal to or greater than | | | Less than | | Equal to or greater than | | |
Industry group	Number	Average price-cost margin	Number	Average price-cost margin	Difference	Number	Average price-cost margin	Number	Average price-cost margin	Difference
Food and kindred products	21	14.08	11	27.74	13.66 [a]	27	16.45	5	31.35	14.90 [a]
Stone, clay and glass products	14	20.60	9	26.37	5.77 [b]	21	21.78	2	34.13	12.35 [b]
Primary metals	10	10.72	5	20.06	9.34 [b]	12	12.02	3	21.08	9.06 [c]
Fabricated metals	16	16.99	4	25.68	8.69	18	17.96	2	25.66	7.70
Electrical machinery	7	19.94	11	25.04	5.10	10	20.04	8	26.84	6.80 [c]
Miscellaneous	20	18.69	3	23.80	5.11 [a]	23	19.36	—	—	—
Textile mill products	15	13.06	2	11.64	−1.42	17	12.90	—	—	—
Apparel and related products	24	15.16	—	—	—	24	15.16	—	—	—
Chemicals and allied products	7	29.65	12	25.66	−3.99	13	28.25	6	24.71	−3.54
Machinery, except electrical	14	17.01	8	21.11	4.10	19	18.18	3	20.54	2.36
Others	55	16.80	20	18.80	2.00	68	17.33	7	17.40	0.07
All industries	203	16.78	85	23.16	6.38 [a]	252	17.81	36	24.61	6.80 [a]

[a] Significant at 1 percent level.   [b] Significant at 5 percent level.   [c] Significant at 10 percent level.

not contain any industry with four-firm concentration as high as 70 percent; differences in average margins for industry concentration above and below 50 percent in this group are, however, statistically significant. For the Electrical Machinery group, differences are significant at the 70 percent breaking point but not at the 50 percent break. The differences for Fabricated Metal Products group are large but not statistically significant at either point. For the other three industries in which significant regression results were obtained, the dichotomous test also yields significant results at both breaking points. For all industries, the difference in mean margins between relatively concentrated and unconcentrated industries is significant at the 1 percent level whether the division is made at the 50 percent or 70 percent concentration ratio. An important factor in this last result is the relative weight of the low-margin, low-concentration Textile and Apparel industries. However, neither the other four industry groups nor the seventy-five additional industries reveal statistically significant differences in average margin levels between concentrated and unconcentrated industries as defined by either of these breaking points.

Further evidence of a distinct break in the concentration-margin relationship might be found at some other concentration level. However, the data in Appendix A and the experimental tabulations by deciles and other class limits do not yield substantially different results. Evidence of a sharp difference between "highly concentrated" and "all other" industries in our data appears to come entirely from industries in which there is also some evidence of a continuous concentration-margin relationship, and from industries clustered in the lower portion of the concentration spectrum. Scatter plots of the basic data, not shown, also fail to produce additional support for the "distinct-break" hypothesis.[5] We are therefore led to conclude that the association be-

---

[5] The figures in this chapter do not bear on this hypothesis. The plotted points are residuals from the net regression, not basic data.

tween concentration and price-cost margins revealed in this data may be described as continuous rather than discrete. This conclusion is strengthened rather than weakened by the evidence of dichotomous differences within larger collections of data, including subsamples that do not span the full range of the concentration variable.

V

Conclusion

Our analysis of 1958 concentration data tends to confirm the conclusions of previous studies indicating a statistically significant, but not always strong, association between concentration and indicators of profitability in manufacturing industries. This association was observed both in aggregate data and in more refined classifications, although not in every subsample of the latter. The association between the two variables, where observed, appeared to be well described in terms of a continuous function. The "distinct break" in the concentration-profitability relationship reported in some other studies was not generally found in these data.

The strength of our findings varies substantially depending upon the profit indicator considered, the classification level of the data, and the subsample under analysis. When data for two-digit major industry groups were analyzed, profits as a percentage of equity, before and after taxes, were shown to be the profitability indicator most closely associated with variations in average concentration levels. However, when capital-output ratios were introduced as an additional explanatory variable, profits as a percentage of sales became the profit indicator most closely associated with concentration. All the more familiar indicators—profits as a percentage of sales, assets, and equity—were more closely related than the computed price-cost margins to these average concentration indexes. Margins were, however, fairly closely correlated with the other profit measures; and the association between margins and average concentration levels in the major industry groups was statistically significant.

When attention was shifted to concentration and margins in the more narrowly defined four-digit industries, widely varied results were obtained from different subsamples of the data. All large samples containing highly diverse industries revealed a significant association between concentration and margins; and in six of the ten subsamples of four-digit industries within the same major industry groups, significant concentration-margin relationships were found. Concentration alone, however, never explained as much as a half, and rarely as much as a fourth, of the variation in margins among four-digit industries.

The central tendency (median) of the significant regression coefficients for the concentration variable, whether or not other variables were included, was .14. (This is not substantially different from the coefficients of average concentration on margins in the two-digit groups—.15–.17.) Even if the four nonsignificant results are included as zero values, the median coefficient is .12–.13. On the basis of these findings we would predict that in samples of four-digit Census industries differences of as much as 10 percentage points in the share of the four largest firms in total industry shipments would most likely be accompanied by differences of 1 to 1.5 percentage points in industry-wide price-cost margins, as we compute them. We should not be surprised, however, if this prediction were wide of the mark in certain instances. The coefficients obtained are only best estimates within a range of probable values, and even the direction of the relationship is not invariant.

For a perspective on these results, note that the median level of concentration among the 288 industries is in the 30 to 40 percent interval, and the median price-cost margin is around 15 percent. Fifty-three, or approximately 18 percent, of these industries had four-firm concentration ratios of more than 60 percent in 1958. And in about 10 percent of all four-digit industries for which concentration data were tabulated, the share of the four largest firms in total shipments increased 10 or more percentage points between 1947 and 1958. Thus neither high levels nor substantial increases in concentration are rare, and the order of magnitude of the predicted margin increases—more than one percentage point on a median of 15—is of more than minimal proportions. The welfare loss owing to monopoly pricing may be estimated as approximately half of the product of the excess profit margin and the reduction in total purchases owing to the higher price.[1] Crude assumptions are required both to specify the portion of the computed margins that is truly excessive and to estimate the amount by which total purchase volume is reduced. However, almost any plausible assumptions would yield estimates of welfare losses averaging 5 to 10 percent of sales for the more concentrated industries. (For any given demand elasticity, the amount of the welfare loss increases exponentially with the excess profit margin.) The aggregate welfare impact depends, then, upon the relative importance of these industries in total manufacturing, and the offsetting effects, if any, that may arise from abnormally low profits elsewhere.

DIVERSITY OF RESULTS

A perplexing feature of our statistical results is their diversity, particularly the absence of significant concentration-margin relationships among the four-digit industries in four of our ten major industry group subsamples. This is particularly troublesome in view of the stronger results obtained from the two-digit group data and the larger four-digit industry samples. In principle, the more accurately industries are defined and the greater the similarity, other than structure, among industries, the more clearly the impact of structural differences should be revealed. A priori it seemed reasonable to expect greater similarity among in-

---

[1] Harberger, *op. cit.*

dustries within the same broad field of economic activity than among all industries or among the broad fields themselves. However, the associations between price-cost margins and average concentration levels for broad industry aggregates are as strong as (and the association between other profit measures and average concentration stronger than) those found in the analysis of more narrowly defined industry categories. This result parallels the findings of previous studies, noted in Chapter II, in which significant associations between concentration and profitability were invariably found from analysis of data at the two-digit major industry group level.

The relative strength of the concentration-profitability relationship in the aggregate data does not appear to be due to any purely arithmetic effect (e.g., effects of averaging, weighting, etc.). It might be thought that profitability would be more variable than concentration among the four-digit components of any two-digit major industry group. If so, the averaging involved in computing group data would result in a relatively greater reduction in variability for the profit indicator than for the concentration index, and thus would strengthen the statistical relationship between them. The absence of rate-of-return data for four-digit industries makes it impossible to evaluate this possibility completely. However, a comparison of the concentration and margin data for two-digit and four-digit industries (tables 12 and 13 and Appendix A) gives it no support. Although not all four-digit industries are included in the Appendix tables, the large collection of data available indicates that concentration and margins are about equally variable within each of the two-digit groups, and thus that averaging would not, in general, affect one characteristic more than the other. Nor do the two-digit group results appear to be due primarily to the role of large industries—either greater weight or market leadership—within their groups.

We are therefore led to conclude that the profits-concentration association among the group aggregates is a real phenomenon, which is not invalidated by our failure to detect a similar relationship in particular intragroup subsamples. One reason that concentration might be more closely associated with profitability between, rather than within, the principal sectors of industry is that the competitive adjustments necessary to equalize interindustry profit rates are apt to be much easier within, rather than between, the sectors. Thus we might expect firms—or the birth and death of firms—to shift resources marginally from one textile industry to another, or one machinery industry to another, but much less readily from textiles to machinery. Similarly, the adaptation of products and market offerings to profit opportunities must be easier within major industry categories than between them. These competitive pressures need not have any effect on measured four-firm concentration within narrowly defined industries. Their effects would be on the ability of firms in more concentrated industries to obtain monopoly profits. The prevalence and strength of these effects depend, however, on the relative importance of unconcentrated industries within the major sector. In a major sector characterized primarily by unconcentrated industries (in which the average level of concentration is low), the potential monopoly profits of the few concentrated industries may be eroded. However, in a sector composed of concentrated industries, this erosion process will not take place to the same extent. As a result, the association between concentration and profitability may manifest itself as an association between average concentration and profitability levels among industry aggregates.

If this argument identified the only relevant considerations, we would expect *no* association between concentration and profitability within the industry group subsamples. Such is not the case, nor should such a result be anticipated. However, this argument does seem to help explain some of the diversity among these subsamples. Modifying our earlier hypothesis, we might expect a major industry group composed of extremely diverse industries with few substitution possibilities between them to permit the persistence of substantial interindustry (intragroup) profit disparities; whereas a group composed of industries with strong resource and product substitution possibilities would not do so. Where interindustry differences are sharper, industry classifications more accurately describe economic reality; and the associations between industry shipments and market size, between concentration of shipments and degree of oligopoly, are therefore stronger.

There is, of course, no very precise way to measure the technological and product similarity of multiple industries. However, the effect of internal heterogeneity on our results for the industry group subsamples is suggested by the lists of groups for which significant concentration-margin relationships were and were not observed (tables 20 and 21, respectively). The groups within which significant associations were found include examples of high internal diversity: Food and Kindred Products; Stone, Clay and Glass Products; Primary Metals; Miscellaneous Manufacturing. There would be substantial barriers to competitive substitution among many of the constituent industries within these groups, even though all or most of them might be subject to similar long-run demand and cost conditions. In contrast, the groups within which no significant concentration-margin relationship was observed include at least three industries in which the possibilities of competitive substitution of resources and products are relatively strong: Textiles, Apparel, and Machinery. Thus we might expect the profits-equalizing force of interindustry competition, or potential competition, to work against any substantial differences in profitability associated with narrowly measured concentration.

The technological similarity of industries also undoubtedly affects the spread of technological change among them. If it is true, as frequently alleged and sometimes demonstrated, that large firms in concentrated industries exercise greater leadership in technological innovation, an associa-

tion between concentration and innovation-based profits
would be anticipated on this ground alone. Further, we
would expect innovative developments arising in the more
concentrated industries to "infect" the less concentrated industries closely related to them; and, as a result, the profit
differences between technologically similar concentrated
and unconcentrated industries would tend to disappear.
Then, if innovations bring profits, unconcentrated industries
in technologically advanced sectors of the economy should
obtain profit advantages over those in less advanced sectors.
If the sectors with high average concentration are also those
with high rates of technological advance, for the reason
cited, we would expect, again, an association between average concentration levels and profitability in broad industry
aggregates.

There is also the factor of international competition, both
actual and potential. Actual foreign sales in the domestic
market give rise to a discrepancy between concentration in
domestic shipments and concentration in market activity.
The potential competition of imports may set a ceiling on
the profitability of domestic firms, even though no imports
occur. In either case, the association between domestic concentration and profitability may be altered. This problem
may arise at both the two-digit and the four-digit industry
level, but is probably most important for narrowly defined
industries, some of which may be subject to keen international competition. If so, statistical results for small samples
containing some of these industries would be substantially
affected, although these effects would wash out both in large
samples and in industry group averages.

Differences in the strength of substitution possibilities,
technological similarity, and foreign competition, although
undoubtedly important, cannot explain all the diversity
among our results. The number and size of industries in each
sample and in each major group aggregate, and the range of
variable values represented, undoubtedly account for some
of the differences. The SIC classification system itself may

be seriously faulty as a source of data for this type of analysis. Many other variables, such as rate of industry growth, degree of vertical integration, character of principal industry output (finished or unfinished, durable or nondurable, producer or consumer goods), structural dimensions other than four-firm concentration, average size of firm, existence of overt restrictions on competitive behavior, and so on, might be introduced. Further, there may be substantial effects owing to interindustry differences in cost structures not reflected in the capital-output ratio or in the elasticity of demand.

Most of these variables are exceedingly difficult to quantify or even to describe accurately in a multi-industry context. We have attempted to examine the deviations among our findings in relation to each of these variables on an *ad hoc* basis and, though plausible associations occasionally appeared, no general patterns emerged. We therefore conclude that there are important subsamples of industry within which the positive association between concentration and margins either does not exist or is fully offset by other as yet unspecified structural or behavioral factors.

TIMING OF OBSERVATIONS

One additional problem in the interpretation of our results is the timing of the observations. Concentration data and related Census information are available for relatively few and widely separated time periods. Economy-wide changes in scale, technology, and tastes, and changes in the relative importance of individual industries seriously reduce our ability to make comparisons among the sequence of Census observations. Moreover, cross-sectional analysis of data from any single Census runs the risk of obtaining results that are specific to that particular period. We noted at the end of Chapter II a tendency for the 1954 concentration data to yield clearer evidence than the 1947 data of an association with interindustry differences in profitability, and we offered a possible explanation for this result in terms of the different cyclical positions of the two observation dates. The year 1958 is cyclically similar to 1954, and thus the similarity of our 1958 results with those obtained for 1954 is a specific confirmation of the concentration-profits association during periods of mild recession. The greater cyclical variability of profits of smaller firms and, by implication, less concentrated industries may, however, serve to wipe out, or conceivably reverse, this association in periods of peak prosperity. It could be, however, that the stronger concentration-profits association found for 1954 and 1958, compared with 1947, is a secular phenomenon and will in future be observed at all stages of the business cycle. It is impossible to determine from available data which, if either, of these hypotheses is accurate. However, the repetition of our present analysis for data from subsequent censuses should provide important additional evidence on this matter. If the associations found here for 1958 are observed also for 1963, the next Census year and a year of general prosperity, we shall have reason to believe that the concentration-profits association is not primarily a cyclical phenomenon.

CONCLUDING REMARKS

Even if the association between measured concentration and profitability were primarily characteristic of the recession phase of the business cycle, it would not be of negligible significance. If concentrated industries fare better than unconcentrated industries even some of the time, and no worse the rest of the time, they will tend to have higher average profits over the long run. Perhaps as a result, tendencies that initially arose from cyclical causes—the greater decline in small-firm profits during recession—might become persistent because of the accumulation and compounding of higher profits in the concentrated industries.

If our cross-sectional results can be projected into a time

dimension, increases and decreases in concentration may be expected to have substantial effects on the relative levels of profits and prices among industries. Thus a tendency for concentration to increase, for whatever reason, in some industries may be taken as an indication that profitability indexes for those industries are more apt than not to increase correspondingly. Although the association between concentration and profits revealed in this research is neither overwhelming in magnitude nor invariant in occurrence, it would account in the aggregate for a significant misallocation of resources and a very large amount of dollar profits. Our results, therefore, would appear to justify serious concern with relatively high levels of concentration wherever they exist and with substantial increases in concentration wherever they occur.

Our analysis also appears to validate the continued accumulation and analysis of concentration data as a significant dimension of industry structure. The generally assumed correspondence between concentration measures and the degree of oligopoly, including the behavioral implications of the latter, is at least in part substantiated by the finding that there is a significant association between concentration and indicators of profitability in numerous and varied samples of industries based upon various classification systems. The other side of the coin is that concentration does not explain everything, and in some cases it appears to explain nothing at all. Thus, not surprisingly, the answer seems to lie somewhere between the extremes. Concentration is more likely than not a significant variable in the analysis of industry profit and price-cost performance, but other variables also are important and sometimes they appear to outweigh or offset completely the effects of concentration. The identification of these other variables and their careful integration into a more refined theory of market behavior remain tasks for future research.

APPENDIXES

Appendix A

DATA EMPLOYED IN STATISTICAL ANALYSIS,
FOUR-DIGIT INDUSTRIES, 1958

1. Industry and four-digit numbers are on the basis of the revised 1957 Standard Industrial Classification. The 1958 concentration data are available for industries as defined for the 1954 Census of Manufactures. Therefore, only those four-digit industries were selected for which the new SIC definitions were wholly or substantially unchanged from the old SIC definitions. Data from two or more new SIC four-digit industries were sometimes combined to obtain comparability with an industry on the old SIC basis. The listing of more than one SIC code for an industry observation (except for the combination of cane and beet sugar industries) indicates an industry combination comparable to a single four-digit industry on the old SIC basis. Certain industries were omitted because of data deficiencies, such as lack of data on value of shipments. The relation between old and new SIC codes is given in U.S. Bureau of the Census, *U.S. Census of Manufactures: 1958. Vol. I, Summary Statistics*, 1961.

2. Price-cost margin =
$$\frac{\text{value added (adjusted)} - \text{payroll} - \text{other costs}}{\text{value of shipments (including resales)}}$$

The numerator is an estimate of the margin between total receipts and total direct costs for each four-digit industry. Value added is obtained by the Census by subtracting from the value of shipments the following costs: materials, supplies and containers, fuel, purchased electric energy, and contract work. From value added is then deducted total payroll costs. Also, subtraction is made of estimates of selected supplementary employee costs, maintenance and repair costs (other than salaries and wages to own employees), insurance premiums, rental payments, and property taxes. Data on the latter costs were obtained from the sample survey "Supplementary Inquiries for 1957," conducted by the Census as part of the 1958 Census of Manufactures program. Data were estimated on the basis of three-digit totals when not available for four-digit industries. The total of these costs in 1957 was related to the total 1957 payroll figure. This factor was then applied to the total 1958 payroll to obtain an estimate of these costs in 1958. Dividing the total margin figure by the 1958 total value of shipments gives the price-cost margin used in this study.

Source of data for value added, payroll, and value of shipments: U.S. Bureau of the Census, *U.S. Census of Manufactures: 1958. Vol. II, Industry Statistics,* 1961.

Source of data for estimating other costs: U.S. Bureau of the Census, *U.S. Census of Manufactures: 1958. Vol. I, Summary Statistics,* 1961, pp. 9–3 to 9–23.

3. Concentration is computed as the share of the four largest firms in the industry's total value of shipments. Data are for 1958 for industries defined on the old SIC basis.

Source of data on concentration: U.S. Congress, Senate, Subcommittee on Antitrust and Monopoly, Committee on the Judiciary, *Concentration Ratios in Manufacturing Industry, 1958,* Part I, 87th Cong., 2d Sess., Table 2, 1962.

4. Index of geographic dispersion is computed as follows: The percentage of each four-digit industry's 1958 value of shipments accounted for by establishments in each of the four Census regions was computed; also, the percentage of United States population in each Census region. The index of geographic dispersion for each industry is the sum of the absolute differences between the percentage of value of shipments accounted for by establishments in each region and the percentage of population in that region. The greater the geographic dispersion, the smaller the numerical value of this index. Data on geographic distribution of value of ship-

ments (new SIC basis) is from the U.S. Bureau of the Census, *U.S. Census of Manufactures: 1958. Vol. II, Industry Statistics,* 1961. (Estimates were made where Census regional totals were not published.)

5. Capital-output ratio is computed by dividing the gross book value of assets as of December 31, 1957, by the total 1958 value of shipments.

Source of data on gross book value of assets: U.S. Bureau of the Census, *U.S. Census of Manufactures: 1958. Vol. I, Summary Statistics,* 1961, pp. 9–3 to 9–23. Data were estimated on the basis of three-digit totals when not available for four-digit industries.

Source of data on value of shipments: U.S. Congress, Senate, Subcommittee on Antitrust and Monopoly, Committee on the Judiciary, *Concentration Ratios.* . . .

TABLE A. DATA EMPLOYED IN STATISTICAL ANALYSIS

TABLE A-1 SIC 20: FOOD AND KINDRED PRODUCTS

Industry	SIC code, 1958	Y_1 Price-cost margin (%)	X_1 Concentration ratio	X_2 Index of geographic dispersion	X_3 Capital-output ratio
Meat packing plants	2011	4.31	34	61.51	9.77
Prepared meats	2013	8.04	17	34.23	8.96
Poultry dressing plants	2015	5.91	12	37.31	8.96
Creamery butter	2021	6.89	11	112.61	20.13
Natural cheese	2022	7.48	35	97.52	20.13
Condensed and evaporated milk	2023	14.15	50	65.54	20.13
Ice cream and frozen desserts	2024	21.39	38	22.93	49.25
Canned fruits and vegetables	2033	20.11	29	54.77	25.22
Dehydrated fruits and vegetables	2034	14.96	45	143.20	19.21
Fresh or frozen packaged fish	2036	10.52	18	51.03	19.21
Flour and meal	2041	10.58	38	52.10	16.78
Prepared animal feeds	2042	15.32	22	20.68	16.45
Cereal preparations	2043	37.63	83	121.62	21.23
Rice milling	2044	11.15	43	108.43	20.25

TABLE A-1 (CONTINUED)

Industry	SIC code, 1958	Y_1 Price-cost margin (%)	X_1 Concentration ratio	X_2 Index of geographic dispersion	X_3 Capital-output ratio
Blended and prepared flour	2045	29.23	75	56.72	20.25
Wet corn milling	2046	28.31	73	131.56	51.41
Bread and related products	2051	19.11	22	14.61	27.93
Biscuit and crackers	2052	31.32	65	29.27	25.70
Cane sugar refining, beet sugar	2062–63	11.10	50	79.84	36.63
Confectionery products	2071	18.98	18	52.18	23.22
Chocolate and cocoa products	2072	19.93	71	132.83	17.63
Chewing gum	2073	41.67	88	92.66	22.66
Malt liquors	2082	28.98	28	39.31	59.77
Malt	2083	17.98	50	112.94	42.82
Distilled liquor, except brandy	2085	34.11	60	33.96	29.68
Bottled and canned soft drinks	2086	23.66	11	16.33	51.64
Flavorings	2087	39.71	55	11.33	52.52
Cottonseed oil mills	2091	4.61	42	104.75	49.65
Soybean oil mills	2092	7.42	40	103.10	23.87
Grease and tallow	2094	15.35	23	29.64	31.27
Animal oils, nec	2095	22.29	41	58.18	23.87
Macaroni and spaghetti	2098	18.84	25	46.21	52.52

TABLE A-2 SIC 21: TOBACCO PRODUCTS

Industry	SIC code, 1958	Y_1 Price-cost margin (%)	X_1 Concentration ratio	X_2 Index of geographic dispersion	X_3 Capital-output ratio
Cigarettes	2111	40.85	79	101.48	10.93
Cigars	2121	25.66	54	71.76	17.38
Chewing and smoking tobacco	2131	32.81	57	82.84	17.90
Tobacco stemming and redrying	2141	2.97	73	132.86	7.84

TABLE A-3 SIC 22: TEXTILE MILL PRODUCTS

Industry	SIC code, 1958	Y_1 Price-cost margin (%)	X_1 Concentration ratio	X_2 Index of geographic dispersion	X_3 Capital-output ratio
Weaving mills, cotton	2211	8.32	25	120.52	53.69
Weaving mills, synthetics	2221	12.23	34	86.80	36.32
Narrow fabric mills	2241	14.57	16	94.97	29.77
Seamless hosiery mills	2252	15.51	23	103.14	32.49
Knit outerwear mills	2253	13.40	7	111.49	14.45
Knit underwear mills	2254	15.37	29	59.81	24.93
Knit fabric mills	2256	11.83	18	79.30	20.08
Finishing plants, cotton, synthetics, nec	2261–62, 2269	10.42	26	84.16	46.48
Yarn mills, except wool	2281	8.38	24	125.29	40.66
Thread mills	2284	12.81	68	84.18	49.37
Felt goods, nec	2291	20.36	45	60.49	32.40
Lace goods	2292	6.12	21	143.28	40.56
Padding and upholstery filling	2293	16.13	25	23.22	40.56
Processed textile waste	2294	10.82	21	81.00	31.81
Coated fabric, not rubberized	2295	14.80	42	78.01	29.97
Scouring and combing plants	2297	10.47	58	123.41	36.49
Cordage and twine	2298	17.74	38	59.81	47.49

TABLE A-4 SIC 23: Apparel and Related Products

Industry	SIC code, 1958	Y_1 Price-cost margin (%)	X_1 Concentration ratio	X_2 Index of geographic dispersion	X_3 Capital-output ratio
Men's and boys' suits and coats	2311	14.61	11	73.29	7.06
Men's dress shirts and nightwear	2321	14.61	16	69.26	7.36
Men's and boys' underwear	2322	14.28	41	73.90	8.02
Men's and boys' neckwear	2323	19.04	17	91.97	7.75
Separate trousers	2327	13.47	9	43.76	7.67
Work clothing; men's and boys' clothing, nec	2328–29	12.31	16	32.59	7.49
Blouses	2331	12.83	10	108.72	5.51
Women's suits, coats, and skirts	2337	13.78	3	106.09	5.38
Women's and children's underwear	2341	15.23	8	91.09	8.22
Corsets and allied garments	2342	23.64	29	77.88	11.47
Millinery	2351	19.06	6	124.79	5.77
Children's dresses	2361	14.90	13	119.92	5.64
Children's coats	2363	12.41	11	138.87	10.41
Children's outerwear, nec	2369	14.81	14	81.95	6.75
Fur goods	2371	13.49	5	138.68	.96
Robes and dressing gowns	2384	16.87	14	103.78	4.51
Waterproof outer garments	2385	16.42	20	101.02	10.02

TABLE A-4 (CONTINUED)

Industry	SIC code, 1958	Y_1 Price-cost margin (%)	X_1 Concentration ratio	X_2 Index of geographic dispersion	X_3 Capital-output ratio
Leather and sheeplined clothing	2386	14.38	18	97.37	10.02
Apparel belts	2387	18.09	21	101.16	10.26
Curtains and draperies	2391	15.52	26	81.83	5.08
House furnishings, nec	2392	14.30	18	53.20	13.38
Textile bags	2393	8.01	40	29.78	20.33
Canvas products	2394	10.22	14	28.41	19.11
Schiffli machine embroideries	2397	21.61	11	136.17	19.11

TABLE A-5   SIC 24: LUMBER AND WOOD PRODUCTS

Industry	SIC code, 1958	Y_1 Price-cost margin (%)	X_1 Concentration ratio	X_2 Index of geographic dispersion	X_3 Capital-output ratio
Logging camps and contractors	2411	11.68	13	96.40	61.57
Sawmills, planing mills, hardwood dimension and flooring	2421, 2426	8.48	8	88.00	25.50
Millwork plants	2431	10.46	8	33.67	20.66
Prefabricated wood products	2433	15.38	28	45.02	13.34
Wooden boxes	2441–42	10.61	19	43.13	31.70
Veneer and plywood containers	2443	12.22	27	65.81	35.39
Cooperage	2445	4.66	45	56.12	23.00
Wood preserving	2491	13.40	32	64.66	42.01

TABLE A-6 SIC 25: FURNITURE AND FIXTURES

Industry	SIC code, 1958	Y_1 Price-cost margin (%)	X_1 Concentration ratio	X_2 Index of geographic dispersion	X_3 Capital-output ratio
Wood furniture, not upholstered	2511	14.81	9	36.67	27.19
Wood furniture, upholstered	2512	15.90	14	18.89	13.47
Metal household furniture	2514	14.52	14	41.22	23.21
Mattresses and bedsprings	2515	16.89	28	10.22	22.37
Household furniture, nec	2519	21.08	43	41.97	8.61
Wood office furniture	2521	16.75	27	38.35	29.36
Metal office furniture	2522	26.21	38	77.72	29.57
Public building furniture	2531	16.23	27	32.46	20.46
Partitions and fixtures	2541–42	16.21	14	40.26	18.98

TABLE A-7   SIC 26: Paper and Allied Products

Industry	SIC code, 1958	Y_1 Price-cost margin (%)	X_1 Concentration ratio	X_2 Index of geographic dispersion	X_3 Capital-output ratio
Paper and paperboard mills, except building paper and board	2621, 2631	20.25	21	13.53	88.71
Envelopes	2642	14.81	30	44.41	28.60
Bags, except textile bags	2643	12.19	26	23.75	25.99
Wallpaper	2644	13.26	41	82.71	55.70
Die-cut paper and board	2645	16.45	40	49.10	32.39
Pressed and molded pulp goods	2646	30.97	69	70.46	55.70
Folding and set-up paperboard boxes; corrugated shipping containers	2651– 52–53	12.60	17	34.17	31.01
Fiber cans, tubes, drums, etc.	2655	4.56	50	36.41	29.17
Building paper and board mills	2661	20.86	42	26.36	88.71

TABLE A-8   SIC 27: PRINTING AND PUBLISHING

Industry	SIC code, 1958	Y_1 Price-cost margin (%)	X_1 Concentration ratio	X_2 Index of geographic dispersion	X_3 Capital-output ratio
Newspapers	2711	23.82	17	16.84	38.87
Periodicals	2721	29.72	31	92.99	11.70
Books, publishing and printing	2731	38.28	16	79.89	16.13
Book printing	2732	16.95	24	56.91	25.95
Miscellaneous publishing	2741	29.19	29	54.32	12.91
Printing: letterpress	2751	16.53	10	44.84	41.56
Printing: lithographic	2752	16.61	9	44.87	28.38
Engraving and plate printing	2753	19.60	28	70.57	30.07
Greeting cards	2771	24.55	45	80.97	12.91
Typesetting	2791	19.72	6	54.65	30.07
Photoengraving	2793	16.47	8	49.82	30.07
Electrotyping and stereotyping	2794	17.41	29	66.13	30.07

TABLE A-9   SIC 28: CHEMICALS AND ALLIED PRODUCTS

Industry	SIC code, 1958	Y_1 Price-cost margin (%)	X_1 Concentration ratio	X_2 Index of geographic dispersion	X_3 Capital-output ratio
Alkalies and chlorine	2812	28.17	64	35.57	31.58
Industrial gases	2813	36.85	79	3.72	106.96
Cyclic (coal tar) crudes	2814	12.79	93	23.71	31.29
Intermediate coal tar products	2815	19.58	54	55.81	109.89
Inorganic pigments	2816	33.60	69	36.97	71.33
Inorganic chemicals, nec	2818	31.69	55	57.02	82.33
Plastics materials	2821	25.89	40	38.63	59.44
Synthetic rubber	2822	21.98	60	91.23	55.10
Cellulosic man-made fibers; organic fibers, noncellulosic	2823–24	31.80	78	123.18	102.68
Biological products	2831	29.97	44	88.59	67.59
Pharmaceutical preparations	2834	51.28	27	75.06	27.62
Toilet preparations	2844	50.97	29	75.11	13.67
Paints and varnishes	2851	22.76	25	36.70	21.69
Fertilizers	2871	14.84	34	57.37	52.51
Fertilizers, mixing only	2872	11.85	18	39.48	27.23
Explosives	2892	14.45	77	12.28	78.87
Printing ink	2893	24.64	53	57.63	20.66
Fatty acids	2894	12.13	72	78.81	73.84
Carbon black	2895	40.23	73	112.09	51.91

TABLE A-10   SIC 29: Petroleum and Coal Products

Industry	SIC code, 1958	Y_1 Price-cost margin (%)	X_1 Concentration ratio	X_2 Index of geographic dispersion	X_3 Capital-output ratio
Petroleum refining	2911	4.83	32	35.19	53.88
Paving mixtures and blocks	2951	21.62	11	28.90	36.63
Asphalt felts and coatings	2952	12.11	37	18.72	36.63
Lubricating oils and greases	2992	18.65	29	52.86	23.46
Petroleum and coal products, nec	2999	18.36	63	45.08	41.26

TABLE A-11   SIC 30: RUBBER AND PLASTICS PRODUCTS

Industry	SIC code, 1958	Y_1 Price-cost margin (%)	X_1 Concentration ratio	X_2 Index of geographic dispersion	X_3 Capital-output ratio
Tires and inner tubes	3011	21.70	74	49.80	39.64
Rubber footwear	3021	21.55	65	104.00	30.24
Reclaimed rubber	3031	17.16	87	74.63	102.81
Fabricated rubber products, nec	3069	15.94	23	51.51	42.29
Plastics products, nec	3079	17.39	8	59.19	28.85

TABLE A-12   SIC 31: LEATHER AND LEATHER PRODUCTS

Industry	SIC code, 1958	Y_1 Price-cost margin (%)	X_1 Concentration ratio	X_2 Index of geographic dispersion	X_3 Capital-output ratio
Leather tanning and finishing	3111	10.94	18	72.76	22.16
Industrial leather belting	3121	21.88	70	53.91	14.89
Footwear cut stock	3131	12.10	19	94.02	12.34
Footwear, except rubber	3141	16.68	27	61.90	9.02
House slippers	3142	15.76	18	110.71	10.17
Luggage	3161	18.86	27	68.16	19.75
Handbags and purses	3171	15.13	10	133.26	6.15

TABLE A-13   SIC 32: STONE, CLAY AND GLASS PRODUCTS

Industry	SIC code, 1958	Y_1 Price-cost margin (%)	X_1 Concentration ratio	X_2 Index of geographic dispersion	X_3 Capital-output ratio
Flat glass	3211	27.79	92	38.59	101.43
Glass containers	3221	25.83	58	18.44	41.66
Pressed and blown glass, nec	3229	25.25	64	46.62	56.66
Products of purchased glass	3231	25.44	45	61.91	30.22
Cement, hydraulic	3241	39.90	32	18.14	132.27
Brick and structural tile	3251	18.10	12	20.20	74.03
Ceramic wall and floor tile	3253	21.06	44	15.42	40.33
Clay refractories	3255	19.20	43	40.89	97.03
Vitreous plumbing fixtures	3261	21.06	54	39.97	57.20
Vitreous china food utensils	3262	17.82	59	82.06	47.34
Earthenware food utensils	3263	8.17	43	43.18	60.06
Porcelain electrical supplies	3264	17.63	46	34.90	59.58
Pottery products, nec	3269	22.33	15	55.46	52.33
Concrete block and brick; concrete products	3271–72	18.23	12	7.66	47.18
Ready-mixed concrete	3273	15.86	4	17.01	8.24
Lime	3274	22.26	38	48.46	8.24
Gypsum products	3275	40.48	88	9.00	72.47

TABLE A-13 (CONTINUED)

Industry	SIC code, 1958	Y_1 Price-cost margin (%)	X_1 Concentration ratio	X_2 Index of geographic dispersion	X_3 Capital-output ratio
Cut stone and stone products	3281	16.14	16	37.54	52.66
Abrasive products	3291	25.81	58	85.14	39.74
Asbestos products	3292	24.52	59	37.34	42.30
Gaskets and insulations	3293	15.41	25	65.64	41.46
Minerals: Ground or treated	3295	28.61	36	15.10	60.73
Nonclay refractories	3297	28.76	62	24.91	78.05

TABLE A-14 SIC 33: PRIMARY METAL INDUSTRIES

Industry	SIC code, 1958	Y_1 Price-cost margin (%)	X_1 Concentration ratio	X_2 Index of geographic dispersion	X_3 Capital-output ratio
Electrometallurgical products	3313	21.37	73	23.16	90.19
Cold finishing of steel shapes; nonferrous forgings; primary metal industries, nec	3316, 3392, 3399	10.78	27	72.23	39.48
Steel pipe and tubes	3317	14.27	37	36.45	29.27
Gray iron foundries	3321	12.64	24	47.69	51.54
Malleable iron foundries	3322	4.11	42	98.08	71.20
Steel foundries	3323	13.41	25	56.49	63.55
Primary zinc	3333	6.53	62	41.99	80.44
Primary aluminum	3334	29.57	91	91.45	98.83
Primary nonferrous metals, nec	3339	30.55	62	44.68	68.70
Secondary nonferrous metals	3341	7.23	26	58.09	17.50
Copper rolling and drawing	3351	13.25	48	74.58	32.95
Aluminum rolling and drawing	3352	12.39	78	17.05	38.91
Rolling and drawing, nec	3356	12.19	43	63.37	33.43
Aluminum castings; brass, bronze, copper castings; nonferrous castings, nec	3361–62, 3369	11.55	16	59.33	40.06
Iron and steel forgings	3391	7.78	32	78.23	43.25

TABLE A-15   SIC 34: FABRICATED METAL PRODUCTS

Industry	SIC code, 1958	Y_1 Price-cost margin (%)	X_1 Concentration ratio	X_2 Index of geographic dispersion	X_3 Capital-output ratio
Metal cans	3411	15.91	80	28.83	35.95
Cutlery	3421	36.50	53	117.29	28.04
Hand saws and saw blades	3425	23.08	49	78.83	45.04
Hardware, nec	3429	18.14	32	60.89	37.19
Plumbing fixtures; plumbing fittings, brass goods	3431–32	17.10	38	35.10	42.67
Fabricated structural steel; miscellaneous metal work, nec	3441, 3449	13.62	16	16.26	21.50
Metal doors, sash, and trim	3442	14.56	10	23.92	25.12
Boiler shop products	3443	11.12	37	13.59	28.00
Sheet metal work	3444	14.74	15	31.02	18.88
Screw machine products	3451	17.51	9	72.03	49.99
Bolts, nuts, washers, and rivets	3452	19.25	17	62.89	53.21
Metal stampings	3461	14.38	12	67.45	38.54
Plating and polishing	3471	20.80	5	51.54	27.75
Fabricated wire products, nec	3481	15.71	13	46.48	31.65
Metal barrels, drums, and pails	3491	12.95	48	20.71	38.27
Safes and vaults	3492	35.40	91	115.24	35.68

TABLE A-15 (CONTINUED)

Industry	SIC code, 1958	Y_1 Price-cost margin (%)	X_1 Concentration ratio	X_2 Index of geographic dispersion	X_3 Capital-output ratio
Valves and pipe fittings	3494	19.95	17	43.08	35.79
Collapsible tubes	3496	14.89	54	76.67	44.28
Fabricated pipe and fittings	3498	18.19	24	47.16	21.38
Fabricated metal products, nec	3499	20.71	19	53.09	27.89

TABLE A-16 SIC 35: MACHINERY, EXCEPT ELECTRICAL

Industry	SIC code, 1958	Y_1 Price-cost margin (%)	X_1 Concentration ratio	X_2 Index of geographic dispersion	X_3 Capital-output ratio
Steam engines and turbines	3511	26.52	87	82.17	20.45
Internal combustion engines	3519	16.47	48	82.17	32.26
Oil field machines and equipment	3533	23.04	29	89.49	44.85
Elevators and moving stairways	3534	32.47	62	75.46	72.42
Industrial trucks and tractors	3537	11.37	52	48.08	26.34
Metal-cutting machine tools	3541	10.94	21	86.96	76.25
Machine tool accessories	3545	18.01	19	82.27	57.17
Food products machinery	3551	21.11	16	52.51	41.63
Textile machinery	3552	10.68	34	92.48	56.00
Woodworking machinery	3553	17.95	39	32.82	28.00
Paper industries machinery	3554	6.72	47	75.05	35.17
Printing trades machinery	3555	17.47	42	84.04	40.19
Special industry machinery, nec	3559	15.87	10	45.95	39.18
Pumps and compressors	3561	15.47	29	56.54	28.04
Ball and roller bearings	3562	18.96	57	89.33	66.80
Blowers and fans	3564	18.67	28	52.63	72.42
Computing and related machines	3571	4.08	77	66.65	54.49
Typewriters	3572	31.01	79	118.61	38.03

TABLE A-16 (CONTINUED)

Industry	SIC code, 1958	Y_1 Price-cost margin (%)	X_1 Concentration ratio	X_2 Index of geographic dispersion	X_3 Capital-output ratio
Scales and balances	3576	25.21	44	76.41	7.98
Commercial laundry equipment	3582	22.55	51	49.22	42.22
Measuring and dispensing pumps	3586	21.94	52	70.15	25.23
Machine shops	3599	20.47	7	37.01	37.79

TABLE A-17 SIC 36: ELECTRICAL MACHINERY

Industry	SIC code, 1958	Y_1 Price-cost margin (%)	X_1 Concentration ratio	X_2 Index of geographic dispersion	X_3 Capital-output ratio
Electrical measuring instruments	3611	19.67	28	65.48	29.61
Transformers	3612	23.40	71	62.72	35.68
Switchgear and switchboards; industrial controls	3613, 3622	25.33	49	55.06	23.89
Motors and generators	3621	17.91	47	76.96	37.70
Welding apparatus	3623	17.49	39	80.47	27.93
Carbon and graphite products	3624	29.60	87	40.40	83.00
Household refrigerators; refrigeration machinery	3632, 3585	17.80	39	61.79	52.28
Household laundry equipment	3633	22.22	71	102.15	20.31
Household vacuum cleaners; industrial vacuum cleaners	3635, 3584	33.61	70	85.03	24.31
Sewing machines	3636	5.71	88	106.23	65.14
Electric lamps	3641	37.99	92	35.73	32.59
Lighting fixtures	3642	17.39	16	45.15	21.63
Current carrying devices; noncurrent carrying devices	3643–44	24.03	17	66.03	26.90
Phonograph records	3652	36.43	76	63.19	20.41

TABLE A-17 (CONTINUED)

Industry	SIC code, 1958	Y_1 Price-cost margin (%)	X_1 Concentration ratio	X_2 Index of geographic dispersion	X_3 Capital-output ratio
Storage batteries	3691	15.97	64	30.93	32.59
Primary batteries, dry and wet	3692	25.75	84	54.43	20.15
X-ray and therapeutic apparatus	3693	24.28	63	52.90	20.70
Engine electrical equipment	3694	20.50	63	98.13	33.09

TABLE A-18 SIC 37: TRANSPORTATION EQUIPMENT

Industry	SIC code, 1958	Y_1 Price-cost margin (%)	X_1 Concentration ratio	X_2 Index of geographic dispersion	X_3 Capital-output ratio
Truck and bus bodies	3713	13.32	21	47.02	23.25
Truck trailers	3715	12.78	52	28.83	19.05
Aircraft	3721	12.01	59	61.49	22.52
Aircraft engines and parts	3722	13.00	56	64.21	17.35
Aircraft propellers and parts	3723	5.98	97	94.05	69.46
Ship building and repairing	3731	8.90	48	52.33	67.64
Boat building and repairing	3732	12.36	18	11.86	25.49
Locomotives and parts	3741	11.30	95	91.14	38.51
Motorcycles, bicycles, and parts	3751	11.26	58	41.93	71.93

TABLE A-19   SIC 38: INSTRUMENTS AND RELATED PRODUCTS

Industry	SIC code, 1958	Y_1 Price-cost margin (%)	X_1 Concentration ratio	X_2 Index of geographic dispersion	X_3 Capital-output ratio
Mechanical measuring devices and automatic temperature controls	3821–22	25.44	28	61.42	27.81
Optical instruments and lenses	3831	17.80	46	99.26	37.71
Dental equipment and supplies	3843	28.45	45	82.42	22.68
Ophthalmic goods	3851	29.17	52	116.74	37.71
Photographic equipment	3861	29.73	65	106.75	44.00
Watches and clocks	3871	13.30	48	75.48	27.15
Watchcases	3872	12.34	57	136.55	11.44

TABLE A-20   SIC 39: Miscellaneous Manufacturing

Industry	SIC code, 1958	Y_1 Price-cost margin (%)	X_1 Concentration ratio	X_2 Index of geographic dispersion	X_3 Capital-output ratio
Jewelry, precious metal	3911	19.12	18	108.40	8.94
Jewelers' findings and materials	3912	13.85	40	146.63	26.67
Lapidary work	3913	14.33	16	122.60	8.94
Silverware and plated ware	3914	20.34	54	130.97	33.45
Games and toys, nec	3941	21.17	13	64.51	18.17
Dolls	3942	16.24	12	133.79	13.65
Children's vehicles	3943	14.42	37	64.08	33.73
Sporting and athletic goods, nec	3949	25.19	41	50.92	13.77
Pens and mechanical pencils	3951	25.60	51	36.23	29.66
Marking devices	3953	20.02	23	43.85	29.66
Carbon paper and inked ribbons	3955	21.56	29	68.10	18.68
Costume jewelry	3961	17.77	12	136.63	12.16
Artificial flowers	3962	19.96	12	109.25	13.51
Buttons	3963	18.03	20	96.08	33.43
Needles, pins, and fasteners	3964	20.76	35	107.14	45.29
Brooms and brushes	3981	23.03	23	65.63	82.09
Matches	3983	25.47	64	63.94	26.16
Candles	3984	20.85	38	89.75	82.09

TABLE A-20 (CONTINUED)

Industry	SIC code, 1958	Y_1 Price-cost margin (%)	X_1 Concentration ratio	X_2 Index of geographic dispersion	X_3 Capital-output ratio
Lamp shades	3987	16.18	20	87.54	82.09
Morticians' goods	3988	19.69	21	29.40	17.54
Furs, dressed and dyed	3992	18.91	25	118.75	82.09
Signs and advertising displays	3993	17.91	5	35.86	26.28
Umbrellas, parasols, and canes	3995	14.87	26	113.32	9.54

Appendix B

STIGLER DATA ON CONCENTRATION AND RATES OF RETURN
FOR INDUSTRIES CLASSIFIED BY GEOGRAPHIC SCOPE OF MARKET

The data tabulated in Appendix B were developed by Professor George J. Stigler in the research study reported in *Capital and Rates of Return in Manufacturing Industries* (Princeton: Princeton University Press, 1963). His classification of industries by geographic scope of markets was not published there, and was made available to us in correspondence. We are indebted to Professor Stigler and his associate, Miss Claire Friedland, for an explanation of certain aspects of their data and for permission to reproduce the particular observations used in our secondary analysis.

TABLE B Stigler Data for Concentration and Rates of Return on Assets, Selected Years, Industries Classified by Geographic Scope of Market

Markets	1947 concentration	Rate of return			1954 concentration	Rate of return			
		1947	1948	1947–48 average		1953	1954	1955	1953–1955 average
National									
Other tobacco manufactures	86.7	6.54	7.62	7.08	79.4	5.53	6.60	7.74	6.62
Tin cans	77.8	7.27	7.75	7.51	80.0	6.33	5.92	6.97	6.41
Tires and tubes	76.6	6.20	6.70	6.45	79.0	4.79	4.62	5.99	5.19
Cereal preparations	74.9	12.10	12.60	12.35	88.0	8.10	8.96	9.02	8.69
Distilled liquor	74.6	10.18	9.89	10.04	64.0	4.81	3.53	4.80	4.38
Motor vehicles, bodies	72.1	12.04	14.05	13.05	88.1	7.74	8.09	14.19	10.01
Smelting, nonferrous metals	69.1	10.06	9.47	9.77	72.2	4.70	4.53	6.76	5.33
Railroad equipment	67.8	5.18	5.69	5.44	76.6	5.06	4.24	3.86	4.39
Sugar	66.5	6.17	4.66	5.42	65.0	3.84	3.99	4.14	3.99
Automotive electric equipment	66.0	11.18	10.80	10.99	62.0	7.42	4.59	8.77	6.93

Source: Unpublished data, George J. Stigler.

TABLE B (CONTINUED)

Markets	1947 concentration	Rate of return			1954 concentration	Rate of return			
		1947	1948	1947–48 average		1953	1954	1955	1953–1955 average
Soaps and detergents	65.1	17.05	5.27	11.16	65.1	6.56	7.78	8.86	7.73
Miscellaneous electric goods	63.0	8.61	8.14	8.38	59.5	5.24	5.91	4.16	5.10
Office and store machines	62.6	13.23	12.03	12.63	64.8	6.18	6.44	7.43	6.68
Glass and products	61.0	9.58	8.01	8.80	68.9	8.08	9.41	12.33	9.94
Carpets, yarn	56.4	12.43	12.89	12.66	55.7	2.46	2.53	4.09	3.03
Industrial and miscellaneous chemicals	54.4	11.85	11.03	11.44	55.1	6.11	7.11	9.36	7.53
Electric generating and transforming machines	52.9	13.20	13.21	13.20	49.5	6.74	8.23	8.03	7.67
Hats	52.9	6.52	2.28	4.40	54.2	1.98	0.35	3.41	1.91
Communications equipment	52.2	5.75	9.38	7.57	41.3	6.34	5.12	5.56	5.67
Miscellaneous stone products	50.7	9.49	9.93	9.71	48.4	5.69	5.34	7.73	6.25
Agricultural machinery	49.8	7.51	9.65	8.58	55.2	4.70	3.95	5.04	4.56
Engines and turbines	49.5	3.90	10.31	7.10	65.3	5.98	5.47	7.02	6.16

TABLE B (CONTINUED)

Markets	1947 concen-tration	Rate of return 1947	Rate of return 1948	Rate of return 1947–48 average	1954 concen-tration	Rate of return 1953	Rate of return 1954	Rate of return 1955	Rate of return 1953–1955 average
Scientific instruments	46.3	9.15	9.64	9.40	47.8	6.52	8.31	8.02	7.62
Household and service industry machines	44.6	12.03	11.97	12.00	44.8	3.71	4.47	5.17	4.45
Miscellaneous foods	43.5	11.34	9.73	10.54	43.6	6.59	6.75	7.53	6.96
Pottery and porcelain	43.3	12.89	11.53	12.21	46.0	2.61	3.44	4.81	3.62
Oils	43.2	16.25	9.05	12.65	43.8	5.00	5.62	4.16	4.93
Motorcycles and bicycles	42.3	12.10	5.32	8.71	50.0	4.63	2.00	3.28	3.21
Clocks and watches	40.7	11.01	9.25	10.13	43.6	5.82	3.20	4.40	4.47
Insulated wire and cable	40.7	10.47	10.53	10.50	48.0	7.73	5.30	8.00	7.01
Cigars	40.6	4.34	5.32	4.83	44.0	4.79	2.61	4.04	3.81
Miscellaneous rubber goods	40.2	10.41	9.58	10.00	33.4	6.30	4.96	7.63	6.30
General industry machinery	39.7	12.32	12.30	12.31	35.7	6.58	6.21	7.36	6.72
Meats	38.6	7.15	5.32	6.24	32.7	4.43	2.60	5.13	4.05
Electric appliances	35.8	12.45	10.00	11.24	50.0	6.18	7.50	7.71	7.13
Jewelry, except costume	35.2	11.07	9.16	10.12	35.2	3.60	3.55	4.10	3.75

TABLE B (CONTINUED)

Markets	1947 concen-tration	Rate of return			1954 concen-tration	Rate of return			
		1947	1948	1947–48 average		1953	1954	1955	1953–1955 average
Drugs and medicines	35.0	10.82	12.65	11.74	30.5	7.21	8.05	10.32	8.53
Periodicals	34.3	8.24	7.00	7.62	29.0	4.36	1.56	6.16	4.03
Miscellaneous textiles	33.7	15.69	15.04	15.36	32.6	2.32	1.24	3.72	2.43
Paints and varnishes	33.5	12.90	9.31	11.10	36.4	5.79	6.29	7.88	6.65
Miscellaneous furniture	33.3	8.53	5.84	7.18	33.2	4.16	4.41	7.29	5.29
Confectionery	32.4	16.55	9.83	13.19	36.4	6.35	6.52	7.60	6.82
Hand tools	32.0	10.72	9.55	10.14	38.5	5.87	6.47	7.35	6.56
Manufacturing, nec	30.3	7.79	7.61	7.70	28.6	4.46	4.29	5.48	4.74
Miscellaneous fabricated metals	29.4	12.85	12.42	12.64	26.2	7.28	5.12	7.27	6.56
Canning, preserving	28.9	7.19	5.26	6.22	32.3	4.28	3.92	5.95	4.72
Motor vehicles, parts	28.3	12.11	13.61	12.86	33.3	7.12	6.06	9.98	7.72
Wool, broad woven	28.1	10.81	10.25	10.53	27.0	−1.97	−3.89	−1.51	−2.46
Leather footwear	27.8	9.43	6.63	8.03	29.5	5.28	5.74	6.65	5.89
Leather tanning, finishing	26.5	13.53	6.83	10.18	18.0	2.12	1.94	4.17	2.74
Wines, brandy	26.4	−8.16	0.33	−3.92	38.0	2.73	3.60	5.60	3.98
Nonferrous foundries	25.7	10.31	9.97	10.14	22.0	6.06	2.48	5.90	4.81

TABLE B (CONTINUED)

Markets	1947 concentration	Rate of return			1954 concentration	Rate of return			
		1947	1948	1947–48 average		1953	1954	1955	1953–1955 average
Miscellaneous apparel	25.5	10.65	4.94	7.80	23.4	2.70	1.77	3.20	2.56
Yarn and thread	25.2	13.65	12.84	13.24	33.0	3.57	1.58	4.10	3.08
Grain mill products	24.9	11.50	6.16	8.83	32.7	5.98	6.65	5.33	5.99
Perfumes	23.8	7.21	8.11	7.66	25.0	6.55	7.60	8.67	7.61
Costume jewelry	23.8	3.78	4.19	3.98	14.0	2.18	2.25	−0.62	1.27
Miscellaneous paper goods	23.4	15.57	10.98	13.28	25.9	7.02	6.56	7.77	7.12
Fabricated plastics	22.2	4.24	4.48	4.36	8.0	3.72	3.40	4.15	3.76
Construction and mining machinery	22.1	13.10	14.18	13.64	24.7	7.66	7.13	8.18	7.66
Miscellaneous leather goods	21.3	6.87	3.65	5.26	24.3	2.71	3.48	5.19	3.79
Fabricated wire	21.3	12.43	12.40	12.42	18.6	5.48	5.57	7.84	6.30
Special industry machinery	21.3	10.88	10.80	10.84	24.6	4.94	4.56	5.54	5.01
Books	20.5	6.69	6.65	6.67	21.0	4.65	5.45	6.86	5.65
Partitions and fixtures	20.0	12.34	8.10	10.22	18.0	3.34	4.60	6.50	4.81

TABLE B (CONTINUED)

Markets	1947 concentration	Rate of return			1954 concentration	Rate of return			
		1947	1948	1947–48 average		1953	1954	1955	1953–1955 average
Pulp, paper and products	19.1	16.65	13.23	14.94	23.8	7.49	7.27	8.30	7.69
Metal stamping	18.8	12.75	12.77	12.76	14.6	6.29	5.34	7.23	6.29
Cotton, narrow fabrics	17.0	9.72	9.07	9.40	13.0	4.05	3.60	3.29	3.65
Knit goods	15.8	11.51	9.36	10.44	17.3	2.97	2.32	3.26	2.85
Metalworking machinery	15.1	7.78	8.13	7.96	17.0	8.66	7.86	5.24	7.25
Dyeing and finishing	15.0	13.78	11.02	12.40	24.9	3.50	3.81	5.85	4.39
Men's clothing	13.9	11.64	7.06	9.35	14.3	3.70	3.29	4.52	3.84
Cotton, broad woven	13.1	21.32	17.81	19.56	18.0	5.18	2.59	3.73	3.83
Women's clothing	7.4	10.87	6.74	8.80	9.0	1.90	2.36	2.94	2.40
Millinery	7.0	4.47	2.08	3.28	7.0	−5.30	−1.86	0.38	−2.26
Regional									
Blast furnaces	48.4	7.50	9.23	8.36	56.0	6.78	4.86	8.35	6.66
Miscellaneous petroleum and coal products	46.6	11.08	9.16	10.12	46.9	5.97	3.64	6.11	5.24
Petroleum refining	37.3	9.17	11.85	10.51	33.0	7.11	5.68	7.09	6.63

TABLE B (CONTINUED)

Markets	1947 concentration	Rate of return			1954 concentration	Rate of return			
		1947	1948	1947–48 average		1953	1954	1955	1953–1955 average
Miscellaneous primary metals	36.4	13.09	13.22	13.61	34.2	7.23	4.89	8.31	6.81
Wooden containers	31.3	9.30	6.45	7.88	24.7	4.96	2.04	5.03	4.01
Concrete	30.8	10.63	12.43	11.53	37.0	6.84	8.44	9.48	8.25
Fertilizers	30.1	10.61	9.08	9.84	30.9	3.89	4.05	3.77	3.90
Cement	29.5	10.29	14.05	12.17	31.0	8.61	10.61	11.26	10.16
Structural clay products	27.7	11.70	12.47	12.08	28.8	5.30	4.50	8.10	5.97
Fabricated structural metal	21.4	18.16	15.04	16.60	20.9	6.64	6.12	5.58	6.11
Lighting fixtures	18.1	6.44	6.22	6.33	20.0	2.67	4.93	6.94	4.85
Heating apparatus	16.8	12.78	11.82	12.30	19.7	5.35	4.56	6.21	5.37
Miscellaneous lumber	9.9	15.33	13.20	14.26	10.3	5.51	6.11	8.48	6.70
Cut stone	8.3	7.36	8.55	7.96	12.0	2.45	−0.18	3.01	1.76
Local									
Dairy products	38.8	8.26	7.17	7.72	37.6	5.58	6.32	5.77	5.89
Bakery products	27.1	10.36	11.35	10.86	30.5	6.49	6.36	7.29	6.71

TABLE B (CONTINUED)

Markets	1947 concentration	Rate of return			1954 concentration	Rate of return			
		1947	1948	1947–48 average		1953	1954	1955	1953–1955 average
Brewery products	23.1	13.81	12.55	13.18	27.9	6.30	5.38	6.53	6.07
Miscellaneous printing	22.7	11.70	10.54	11.12	22.9	6.82	6.34	7.07	6.74
Newspapers	20.9	11.77	9.88	10.82	18.0	6.66	6.43	8.61	7.23
Iron and steel foundries	19.8	12.01	12.08	12.04	27.1	6.27	4.92	7.74	6.31
Miscellaneous machinery	17.8	9.19	10.54	9.86	13.6	6.59	5.55	6.70	6.28
Nonalcoholic beverages	10.4	8.13	6.03	7.08	10.0	6.13	5.66	6.57	6.12
Commercial printing	10.0	12.68	10.58	11.63	9.4	5.83	5.65	6.60	6.03

INDEX

INDEX